W9-AAH-404

Following Directions

Following directions is a life skill. Everyone needs to be able to follow directions and to give directions. The ideas in this resource book focus on helping young learners to:

- listen to and follow oral directions accurately,

- interpret cues to follow pictured directions,

- read simple written directions, and

- give oral directions for completing a task.

Table of Contents

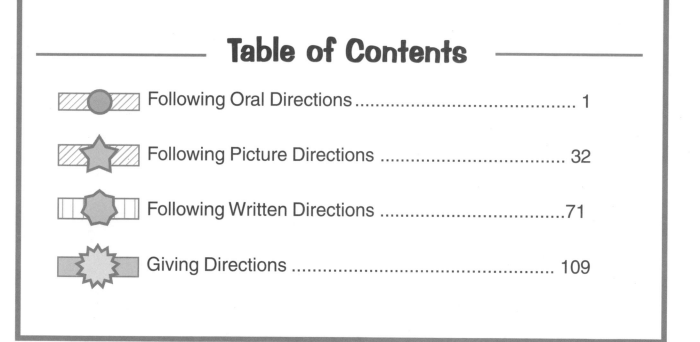
Congratulations on your purchase of some of the finest teaching materials in the world.

For information about other Evan-Moor products, call 1-800-777-4362 or FAX 1-800-777-4332

http://www.evan-moor.com

Entire contents copyright ©1998 by EVAN-MOOR CORP.
18 Lower Ragsdale Drive, Monterey, CA 93940-5746

Author: Jill Norris
Editor: Marilyn Evans
Illustrator: Cindy Davis
       Leslie Tryon
Desktop: Cheryl Puckett

Evan-Moor
EDUCATIONAL PUBLISHERS
EMC 738

Learning to Listen

1. Discuss what listening is. Help students to see that active listening involves more than just hearing something. It involves using eyes, ears, and minds.

2. Develop **guidelines for active listening**. These might include:
   - When someone is talking to you, look at them.
   - Stop moving. Stand or sit still while you listen.
   - Think about what you are hearing.
   - Practice saying directions in your own words after you hear them.

3. Establish a **listening position**. Then you can have learners practice or check their "positions" when it's time to listen.

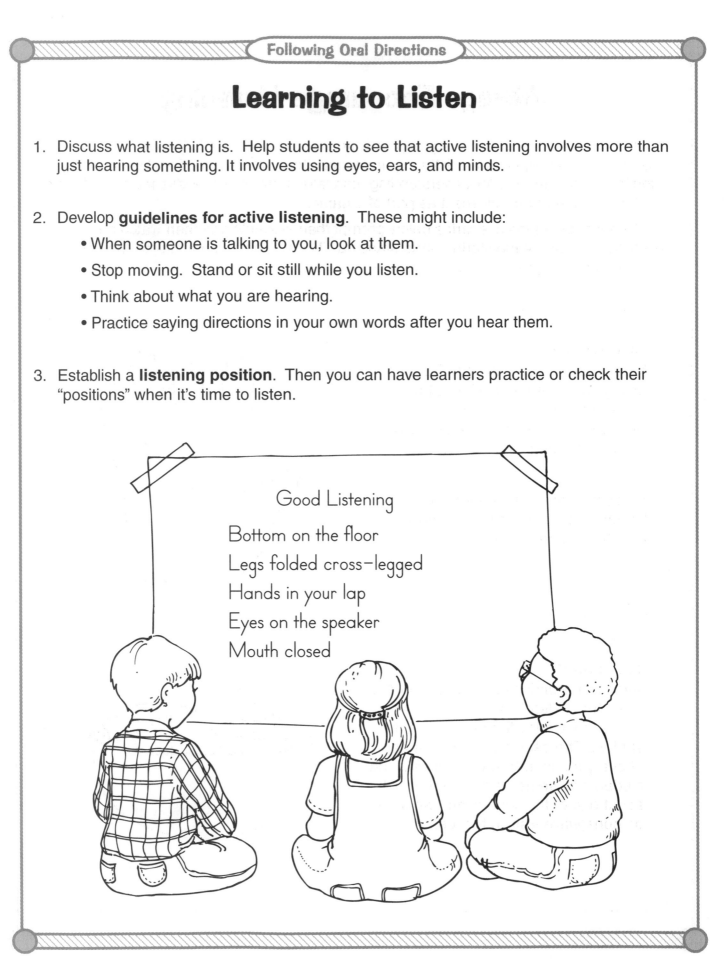

Good Listening

Bottom on the floor
Legs folded cross-legged
Hands in your lap
Eyes on the speaker
Mouth closed

Always Encourage Listening

Whether you are doing a whole group activity or working with an individual, it is important to expect good listening and to monitor to make sure that it is occurring. Monitoring, or checking for understanding, can take many forms. Make it a part of your routine. Your learners will see it as part of a game.

As the teachers in the scenarios below prompt their students and then watch their responses, they are monitoring understanding. The teachers can make on-the-spot adjustments and give individual attention as needed.

Give Me Five

Mrs. Bennett raises an open hand and says, "Give me five." It is her signal for listening. The five fingers represent the five criteria that she has established for good listening.

Students quickly raise their open hands in response to let her know that they are ready to listen.

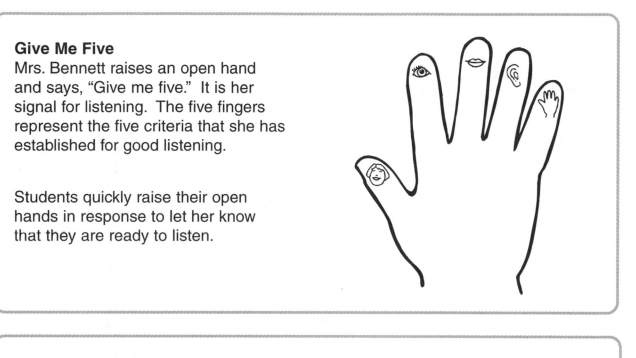

The Basket

After she describes the centers for the day, Mrs. Watson draws a card from a basket containing the name of each student. The basket contains the name of every student. Mrs. Watson asks the student whose name she drew to tell about one of the centers and what can be done while visiting that center.

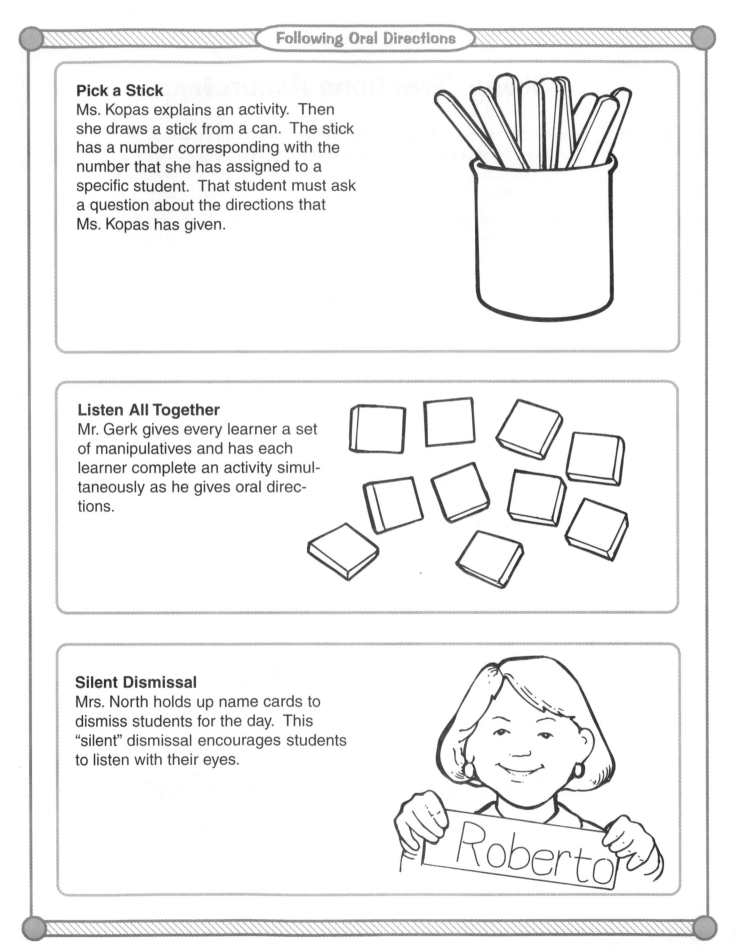

Pick a Stick

Ms. Kopas explains an activity. Then she draws a stick from a can. The stick has a number corresponding with the number that she has assigned to a specific student. That student must ask a question about the directions that Ms. Kopas has given.

Listen All Together

Mr. Gerk gives every learner a set of manipulatives and has each learner complete an activity simultaneously as he gives oral directions.

Silent Dismissal

Mrs. North holds up name cards to dismiss students for the day. This "silent" dismissal encourages students to listen with their eyes.

Giving Directions Accurately

Very often, we expect listeners to interpret incomplete or inaccurate directions. As a direction giver, make sure that you are concise and organized.

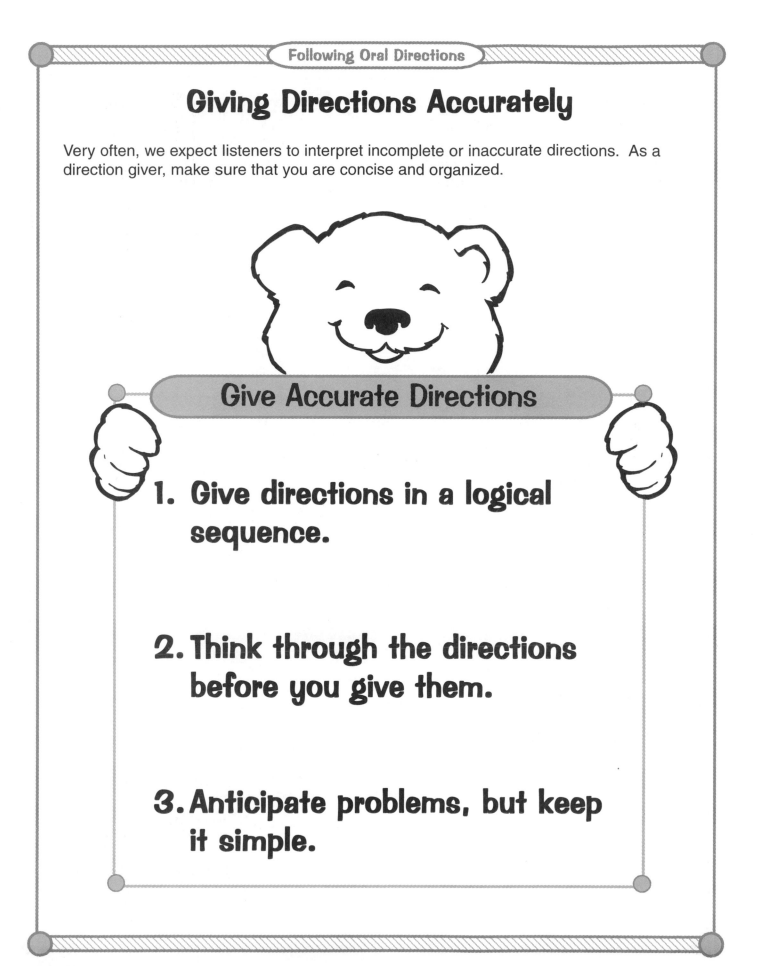

Give Accurate Directions

1. Give directions in a logical sequence.

2. Think through the directions before you give them.

3. Anticipate problems, but keep it simple.

Following Directions • EMC 738

Sing and Chant Directions

Young learners love to sing and follow the directions of a favorite song. Many traditional children's songs are good exercises in listening. Teach these songs to your learners. Then sing them often.

Clap Your Hands

Clap, clap, clap your hands.
Clap your hands together.
Clap, clap, clap your hands.
Clap your hands like this.

Repeat with wave your arms, stamp your feet, nod your head, blink your eyes, and turn around. Then make up verses of your own.

Put Your Finger in the Air

Put your finger in the air, in the air.
Put your finger in the air, in the air.
Put your finger in the air.
Tell me how's the air up there.
Put your finger in the air, in the air.

Repeat with elbow, nose, knee, toe, etc.

Hokey Pokey

You put your right hand in.
You put your right hand out.
You put your right hand in
And you shake it all about.
Do the hokey pokey
And turn yourself around
That's what it's all about.

And it continues with -- left hand, right foot,
left foot, knees, elbows, head, backside,
whole self

Stand Up

(Sing this verse to the chorus of "My Bonnie
Lies Over the Ocean")

Stand up. Stand up. Stand up
and take a bow, a bow.

Stand up. Stand up. Stand Up
Now you can show us how.

Variations: Sit down. Bend low. Stretch
high. Hop fast. Kick front. Kick back.

Try chanting these directions.

Kick your left foot.
Now your right.
Now again with
All your might.

Shake your left hand.
Now your right.
Now again with
All your might.

Stomp your left foot.
Now your right.
Now again with
All your might.

Variations:

Wave your right finger.
Lift your right shoulder.
Bend your left knee.
Circle your left arm.
Shake your left foot.

One-and-Two-Action Commands

Reproduce this page. Cut the slips apart. Put them into a basket or bowl. Each student draws a slip, teacher reads the directions, and the student does what the directions say.

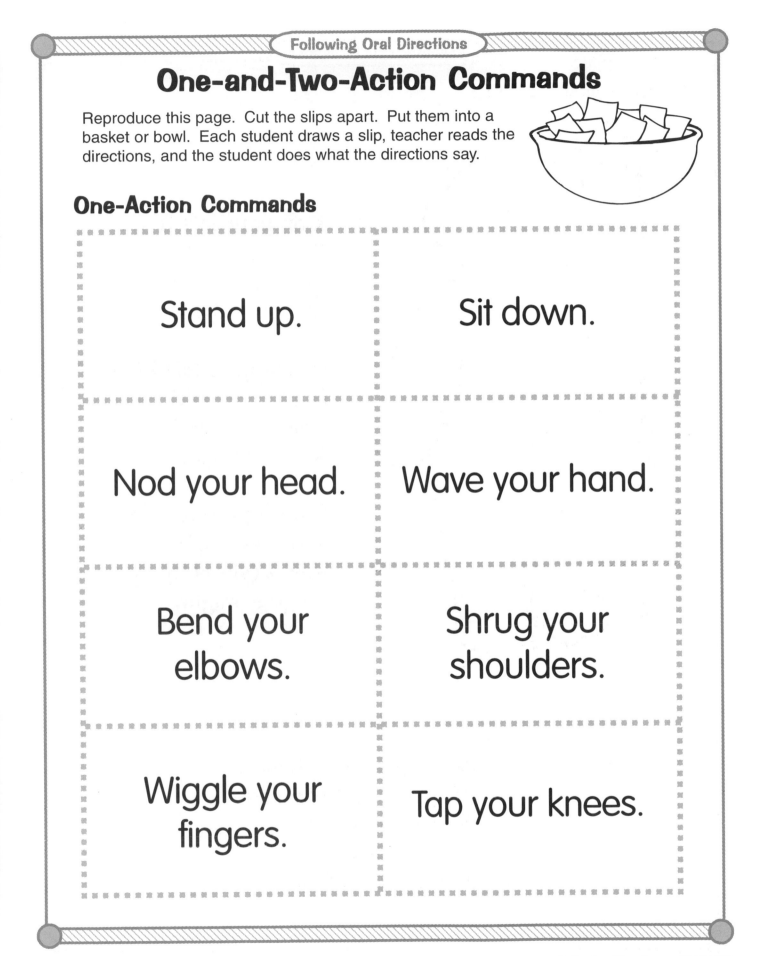

One-Action Commands

Stand up.	Sit down.
Nod your head.	Wave your hand.
Bend your elbows.	Shrug your shoulders.
Wiggle your fingers.	Tap your knees.

Two-Action Commands

Hop up and down and nod your head.

Put your hand behind your back and wave.

Clap your hands and tap your toes.

Kick your feet and shake your hands.

Snap your fingers and walk away.

Click your tongue and sway back and forth.

Wiggle your knees and blink your eyes.

Stamp your foot and tap your head.

Listen and Erase

Make a transparency of the picture on page 12. Project it onto a chalkboard or a dry erase board. Trace the lines with chalk or dry erase markers. Then follow the directions below.

Here's what to say:
"Each time I stop in the story, think of a rhyming word that names part of the hiker. I will erase that part before the story continues."

One sunny day, a little hiker started off on a walk.

He walked fast. He walked quick.
(Stop here and erase the stick)

He followed the route that he had planned.
(Stop here and erase the hand)

The hiker walked until he met a cat.
(Stop here and erase the hat)

The cat meowed. It meant no harm.
(Stop here and erase the arm)

It ran off the path going south.
(Stop here and erase the mouth)

Soon the hiker decided to turn back.
(Stop here and erase the pack)

He was beginning to worry. What could he do?
(Stop and erase a shoe)

What was left in his place?
(Stop and erase the face.)

A simple warning to all who hike alone.
(Stop sign)

"That's the end of the story. The part that's left stands for a warning to anyone who would hike along. What is it?"

The Hiker

Listen and Build

Reproduce the scarecrow parts on pages 14 and 15. Color the parts and laminate them. Add a small strip of magnetic tape to the back of each shape. Line the parts up where they can be seen. Then follow the directions to build a scarecrow.

Let's build a scarecrow.
And watch the corn grow.

Add a part that rhymes with most. *(Post)*

Add a part that rhymes with hurt. *(Shirt)*

Add a part that rhymes with ants. *(Pants)*

Add a part that rhymes with red. *(Head)*

Add a part that rhymes with lands. *(Hands)*

Add a part that rhymes with cat. *(Hat)*

Add a part that rhymes with rocket. *(Pocket)*

Add a part that rhymes with complete. *(Straw feet)*

Now the scarecrow is all made.
Those naughty crows will be afraid.

Note: Reproduce these parts to make the scarecrow used on page 13.

The Scarecrow

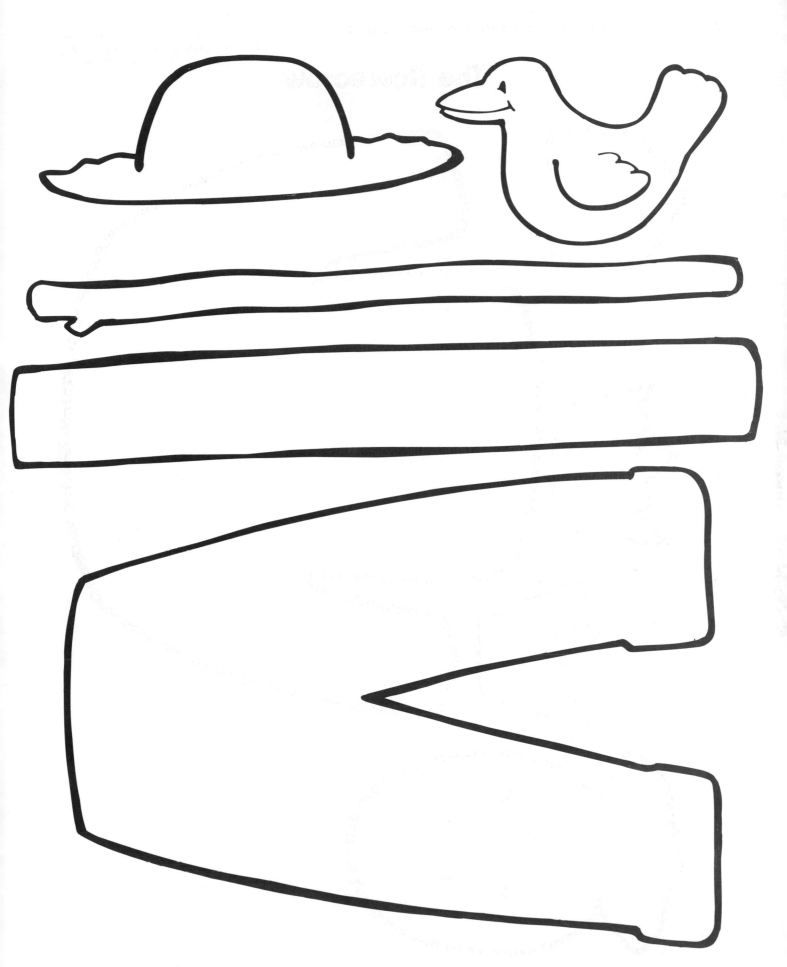

15

Following Directions • EMC 738

This Little Piggy

Use the pattern on page 17 to follow directions with a familiar rhyme.

1. Reproduce the pattern.
2. Color the pictures.
3. Cut out the pictures and the foot.
4. Paste the pictures to the foot.

Recite the poem as you point to each picture in order. When you are sure that your students are familiar with the rhyme and the sequence of piggies, give them directions to follow, for example:

"Show me the pig who cried all the way home."

"Show me the pig who had roast beef."

"Put your finger on the second pig."

This little piggy went to market.

This little piggy stayed home.

This little piggy had roast beef.

This little piggy had none.

And this little piggy cried

"Wee, wee, wee" all the way home.

     Following Directions • EMC 738

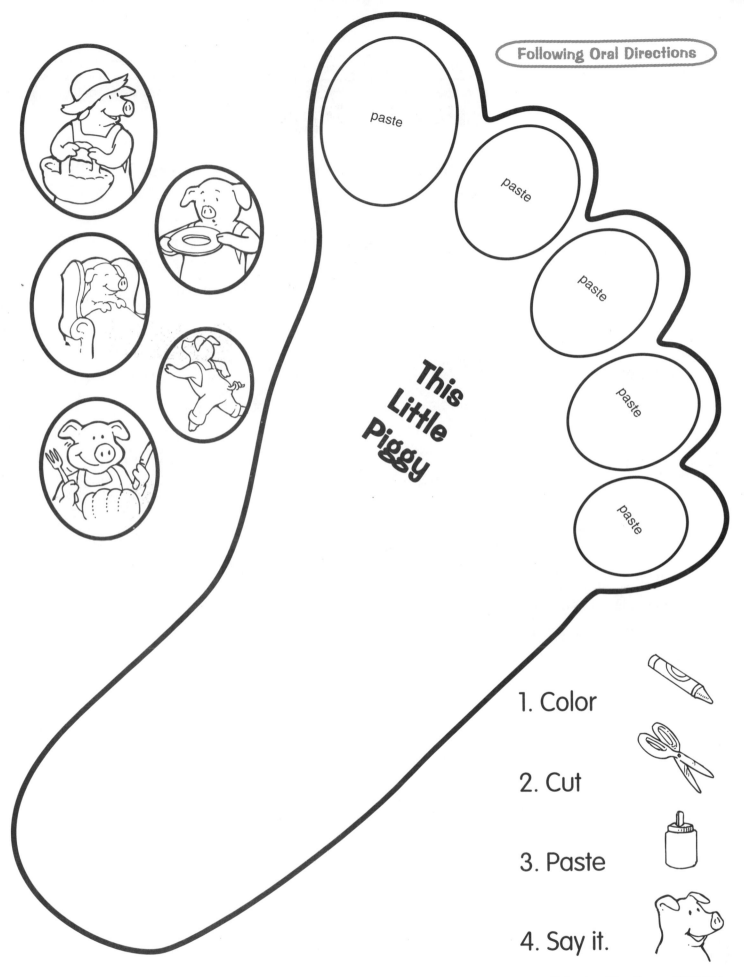

This
Little
Piggy

paste
paste
paste
paste
paste

1. Color

2. Cut

3. Paste

4. Say it.

Picture Bingo

Create bingo cards using the card form (page 29) and the small pictures on page 30 and 31.

Making the Picture Bingo Cards

1. Reproduce one form and one page of pictures for each bingo card.

2. Cut the pictures apart and paste them in random order on the forms.

3. Laminate the bingo cards so that you can reuse them often.

4. Reproduce another set of pictures, cut them apart, and place them in a basket to draw from.

Following Directions Using Bingo Cards

Listen and Cover

(This is simply BINGO using the small picture cards instead of numbers.)

1. Distribute picture bingo cards and markers (beans work well) to students.

2. Draw small picture cards from the basket. Say, "Cover the (dog) on your card."

3. Students use beans to cover the matching picture on their cards.

Listen for Its Sound

Play Listen and Cover, but instead of saying the name of the animal picture, say "cover the animal whose name begins with the same sound as (_____)."

What Do You Do?

Play Listen and Cover, but tell what you do with the toy instead of naming it.

(You can build a tower with these.)

Listen and Match It Center

1. Place assorted bingo cards and a basket containing several sets of the small laminated picture squares in a center.

2. Children take a bingo card and take turns drawing a picture square from the basket.

3. The child taking the turn says "Do you have a _____?" (naming the picture drawn). The child to the right either claims the picture card and covers the matching picture on his/her card or discards the picture card if not needed.

4. The first child to match four in a row or (for a longer game) to match the entire card is the winner.

Picture Bingo

paste	paste	paste	paste
paste	paste	paste	paste
paste	paste	paste	paste
paste	paste	paste	paste

Reproduce this page to use in making animal bingo cards.

Reproduce this page to use in making toy bingo cards.

Teacher Directions for Student Worksheets

To complete the worksheets on pages 24-31, students follow the oral directions given by the teacher, an adult helper, or a cross-age tutor.

Page 24

Materials:

• worksheet on page 24
• crayons

Oral Directions:

1. Put sand on the bottom of the bowl.
2. Add 3 green plants.
3. Put in 3 small red fish.
4. Add 2 large goldfish.
5. Draw a snail crawling on the glass.
6. Put water in your bowl.

Page 25

Materials:

• worksheet on page 25
• crayons

Oral Directions:

1. Make the coat red. Draw a box around it.
2. Make the bird green. Put an x on it.
3. Make the boat blue and yellow.
4. Make the sock purple.
5. Make the whale black and white. Draw a circle around it.

Page 26

Materials:

• worksheet on page 26
• crayons

Oral Directions:

1. Give your monster three purple eyes.
2. Add a strange nose.
3. Put on big, pointed ears.
4. Add a mouth with sharp teeth.
5. Put on orange hair.
6. Now give it spots all over.
7. Be ready to tell your monster's name and where it might live.

Page 27

Materials:

• worksheet on page 27
• pencils or crayons

Oral Directions:

1. Put your finger on the circle in the first box. Draw to turn that shape into a person.
2. Make the next circle into some kind of food.
3. Go to the next row. Make the first circle into something you could ride.
4. Make the last circle into an animal.

Page 28

Materials:

- worksheet on page 28
- crayons

Oral Directions:

1. Draw a fence next to the barn.
2. Put a cow behind the fence.
3. Add a chicken in front of the fence.
4. Put a puppy sleeping by the barn door.

Page 29

Materials:

- worksheet on page 29
- crayons, scissors, glue
- white drawing paper

Oral Directions:

1. Color the shapes.
2. Cut them out.
3. Paste the shapes on another sheet of paper to make and unusual creature.

Page 30

Materials

- worksheet on page 30
- crayons

Oral Directions

1. Make a hole in the tree.
2. Show a squirrel peeking out.
3. Draw some leaves on and under the tree. Make them pretty colors.
4. Make a sun and three clouds in the sky.
5. Draw yourself raking the leaves.

Page 31

Materials:

- worksheet on page 31
- crayon and pencil

Oral Directions:

1. Start at the entrance to the zoo. Draw a line with your pencil as you go.
2. Go inside. Stop to feed the elephant.
3. Turn around and walk to the lion's cage. Color the lion yellow and brown.
4. Turn and walk to the bears. Color the large bear brown. Make the small one black.
5. Walk over to the rhino's pen. Make a black mark on his horn.
6. Now go to see the giraffe. Color his spots.
7. Go past the deer and the zebra. Keep going to the last cage. What do you see?

My Pet Fish

I followed directions to do this paper.

Name: _____

The Closet

I followed directions to do this paper.

Name: _____

The Monster

I followed directions to do this paper.

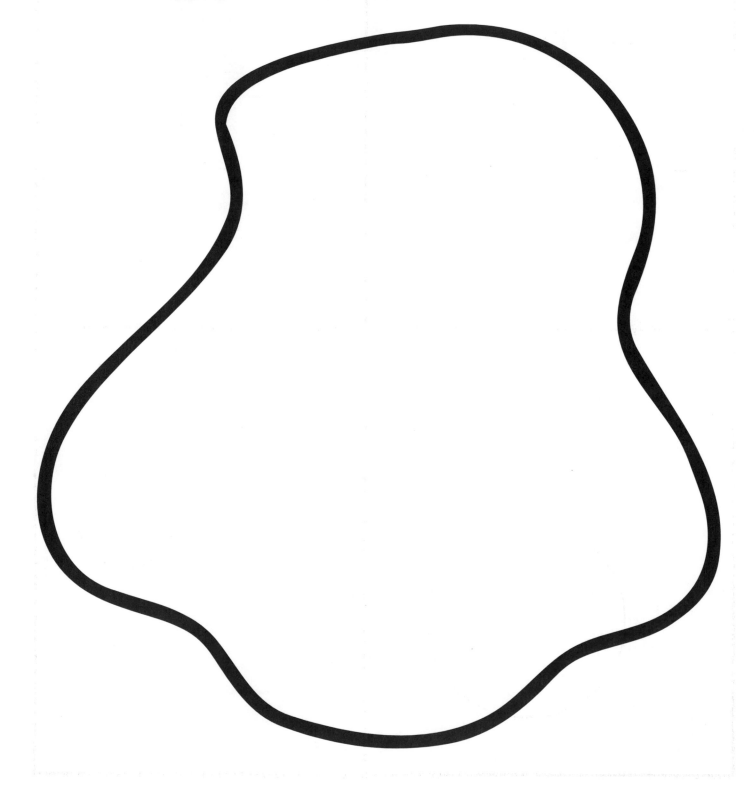

Name: _____

Draw It

I followed directions to do this paper.

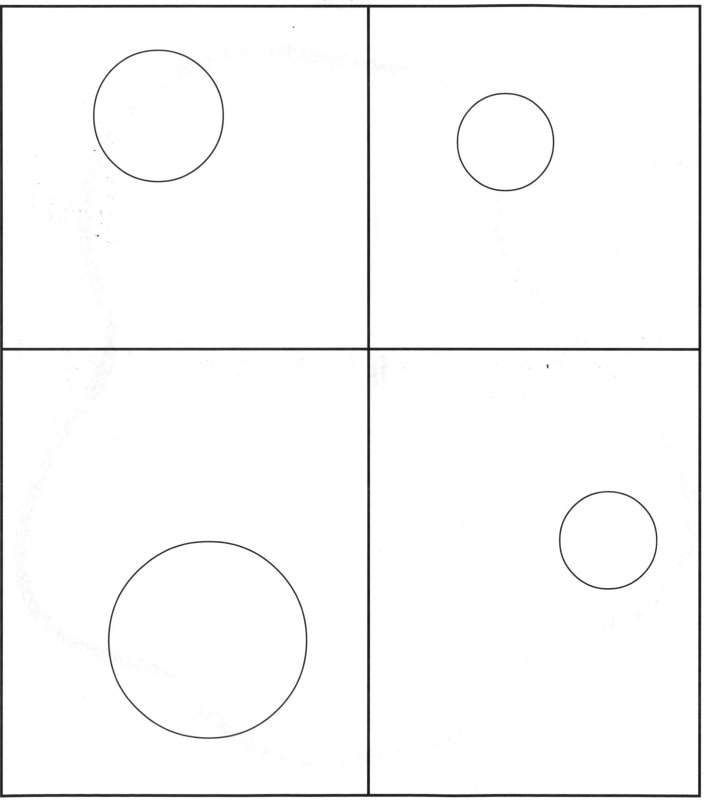

On the Farm

I followed directions to do this paper.

Name: _____

An Unusual Creature

I followed directions to do this paper.

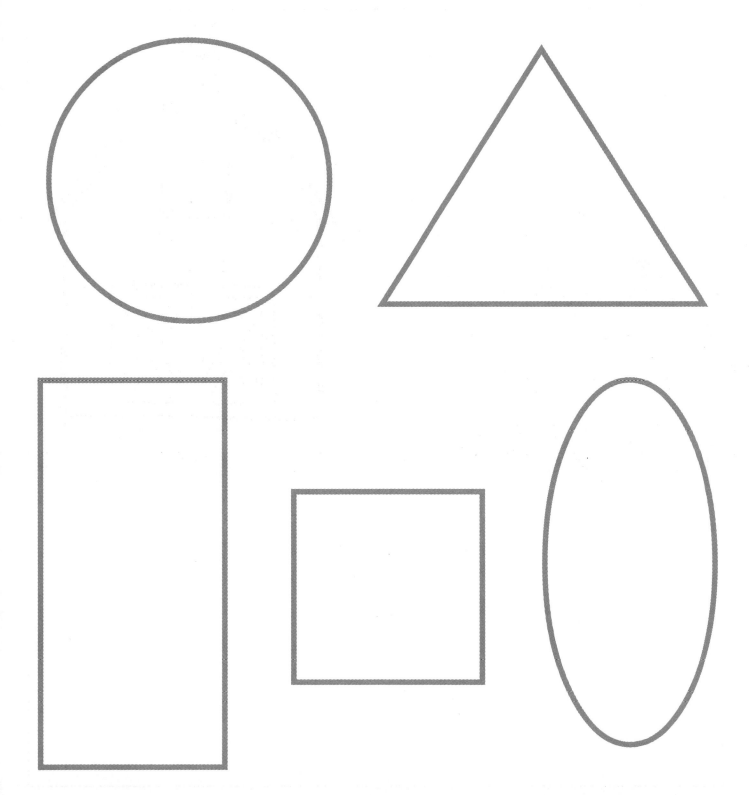

Autumn Fun

I followed directions to do this paper.

At the Zoo

I followed directions to do this paper.

Following Picture Directions

This section includes:

Picture Card Prompts

Picture Card Prompts

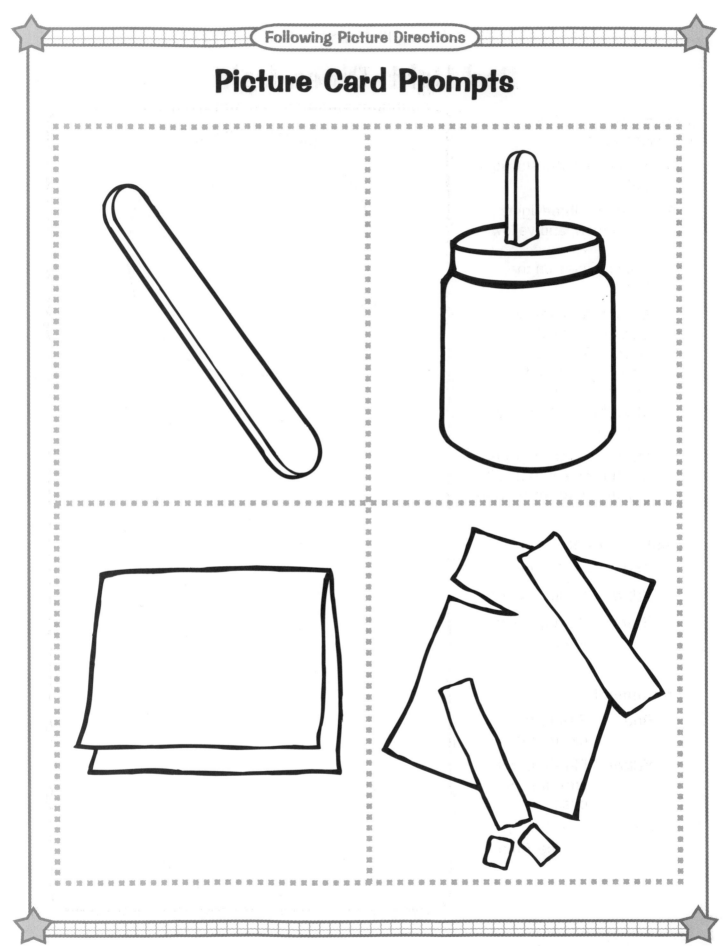

Red Light, Green Light

Make a signal light for your classroom.

1. Reproduce the stoplight pattern.

2. Color the three lights red, green, and yellow or glue construction paper circles on the lights.

3. Cut three circles of black construction paper. Fold back a small section on the top of each circle. Glue this section to the "lights."

4. Post the large stoplight in your room and use it to signal behaviors such as:

• **Talking Levels**

Red	No talking.
Yellow	Whispers only.
Green	It's a good time to talk.

• **Movement**

Red	Return to circle area.
Yellow	Finish up, job time is almost over.
Green	Job Time or Choice Time

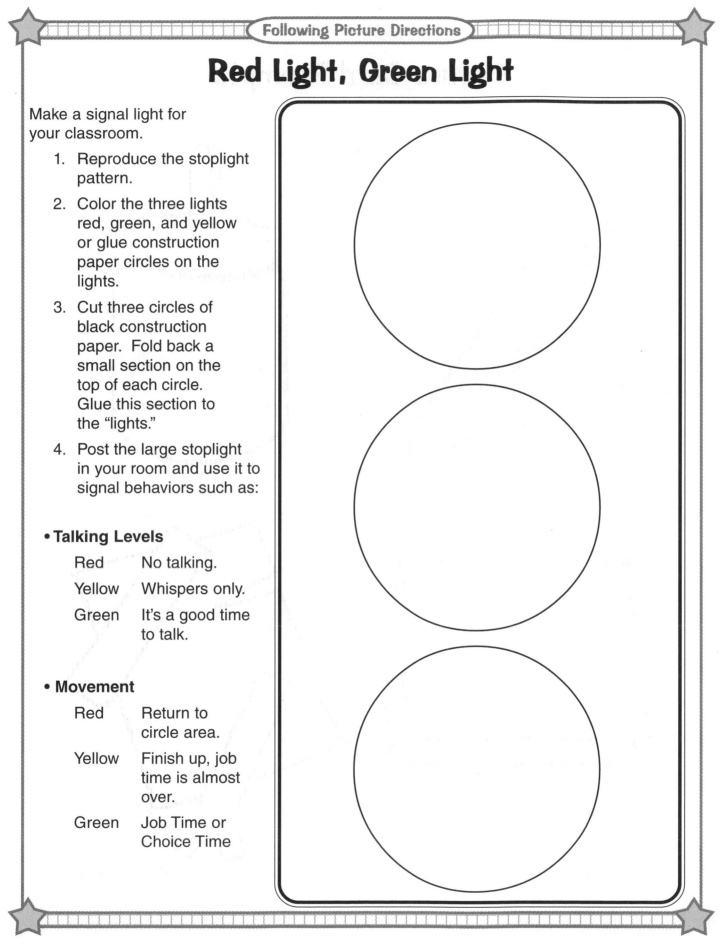

Picture Cues Around You

Signs posted in your school and your community give people directions. Take a walking trip around your neighborhood to identify signs and to practice following their directions. When you return, use the sign cards to model following directions in the classroom.

Note: Reproduce this pattern to use with your building blocks.

Following Picture Directions

Castle

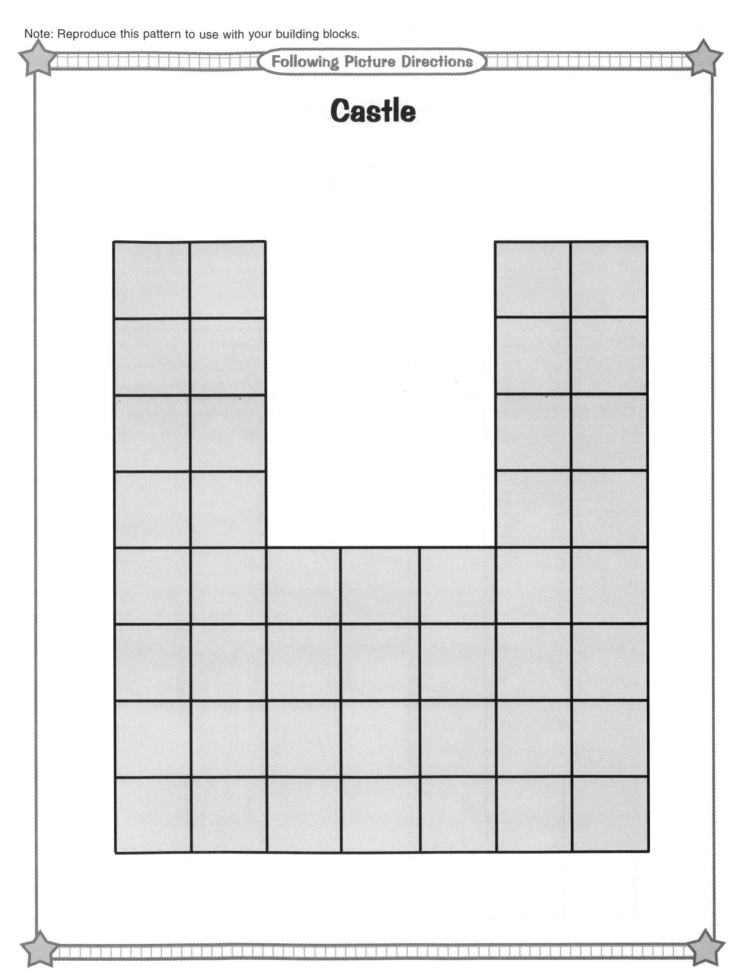

Tall Tower

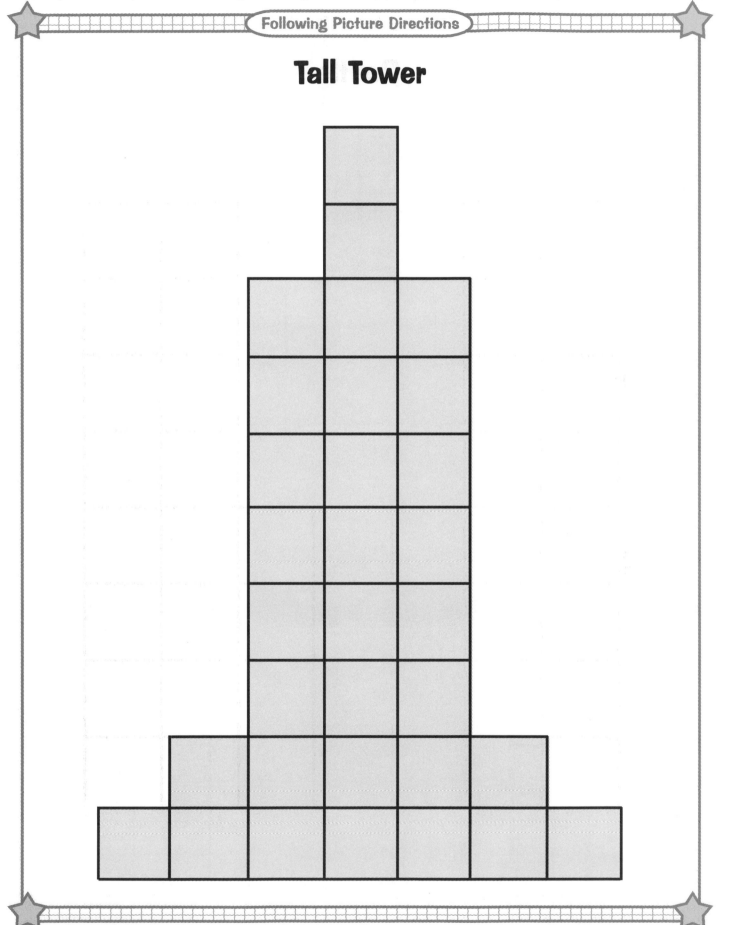

Giant Arch

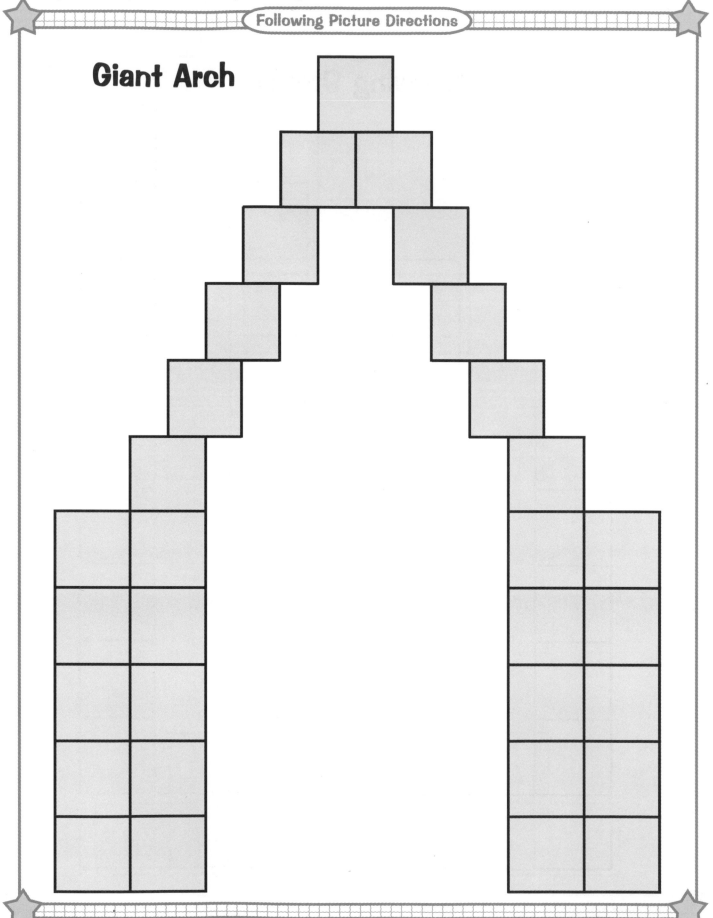

Growing Stacks

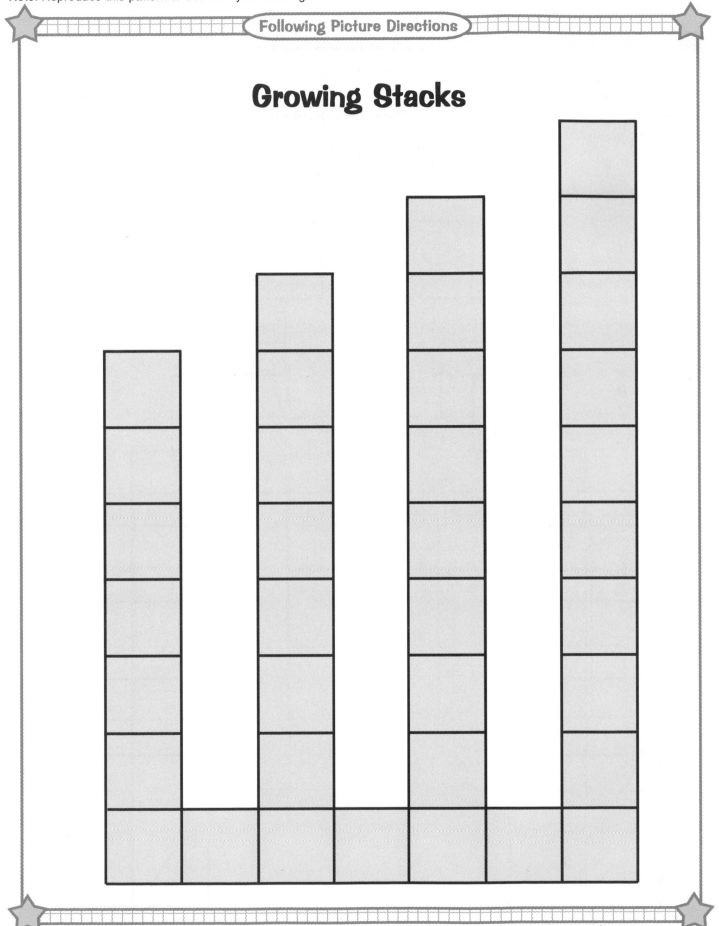

Fancy Fence

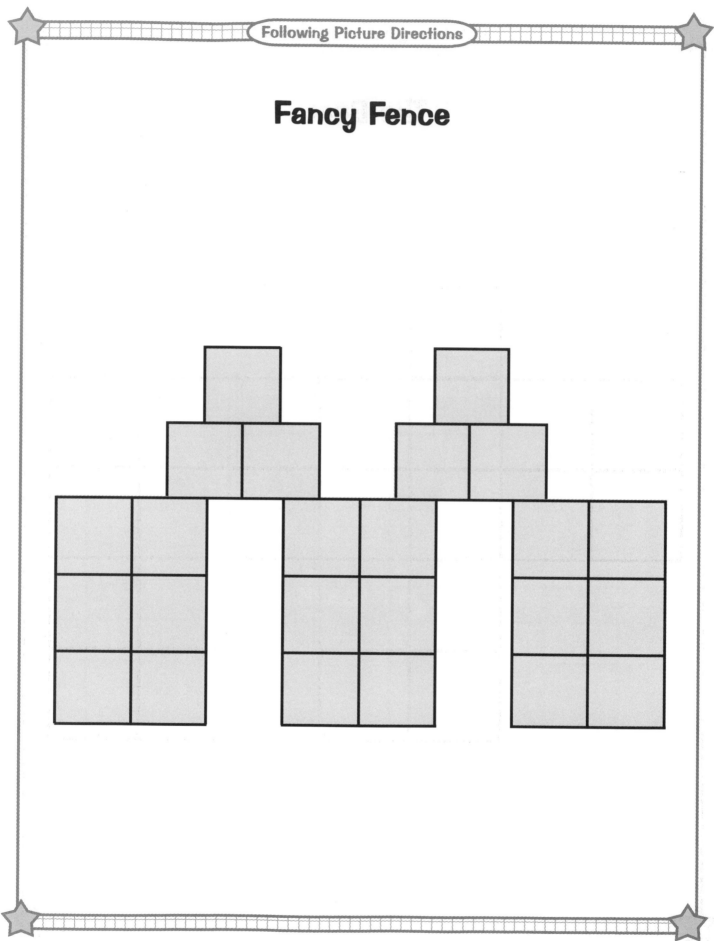

The Bear

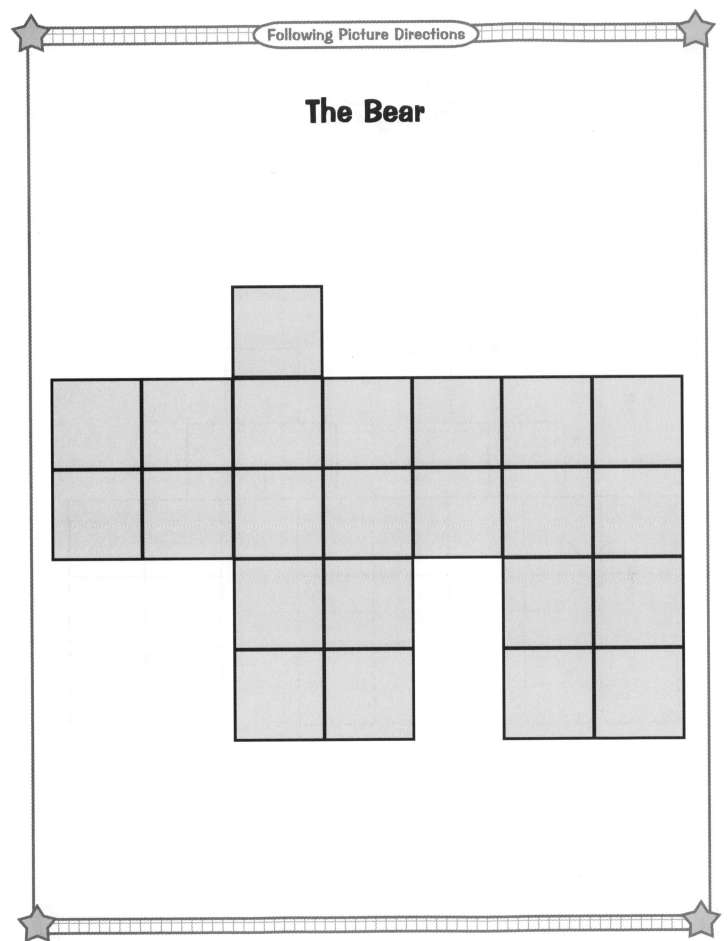

The Truck

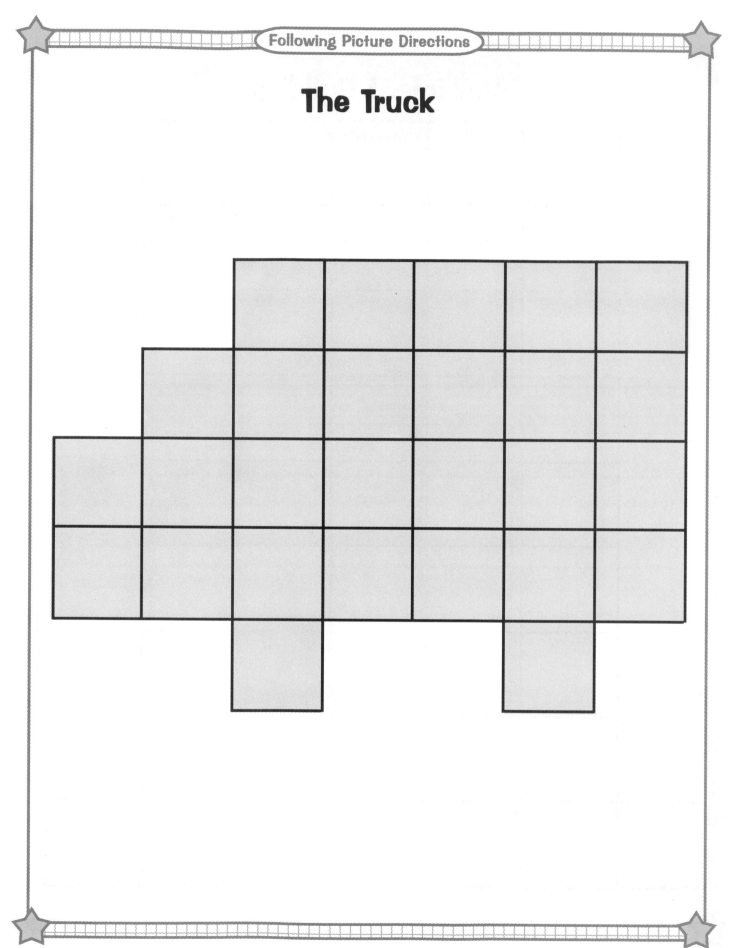

Apartment Building

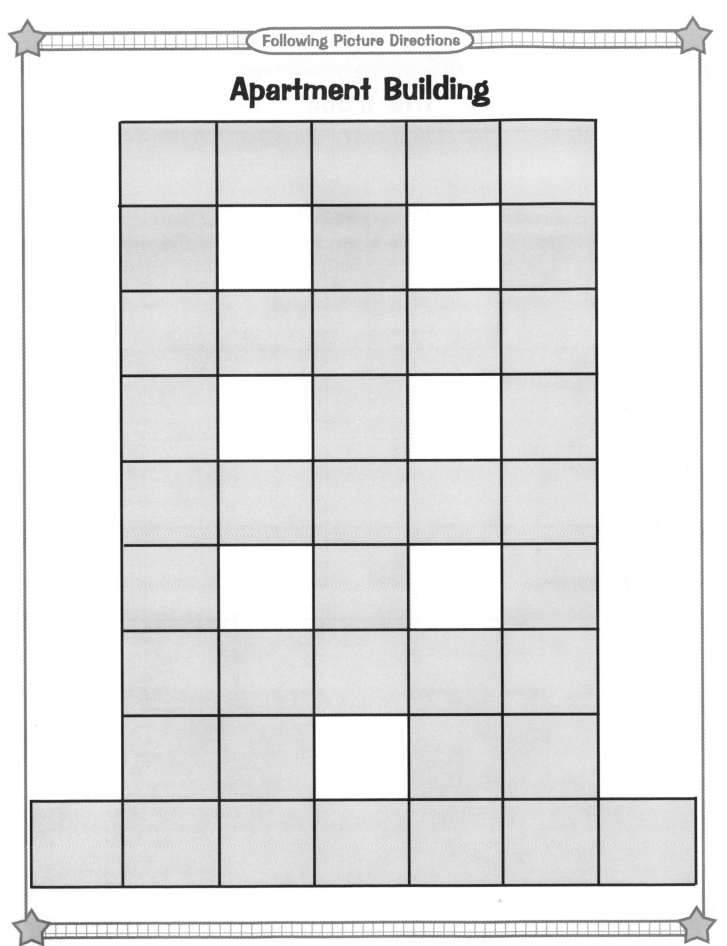

The Robot

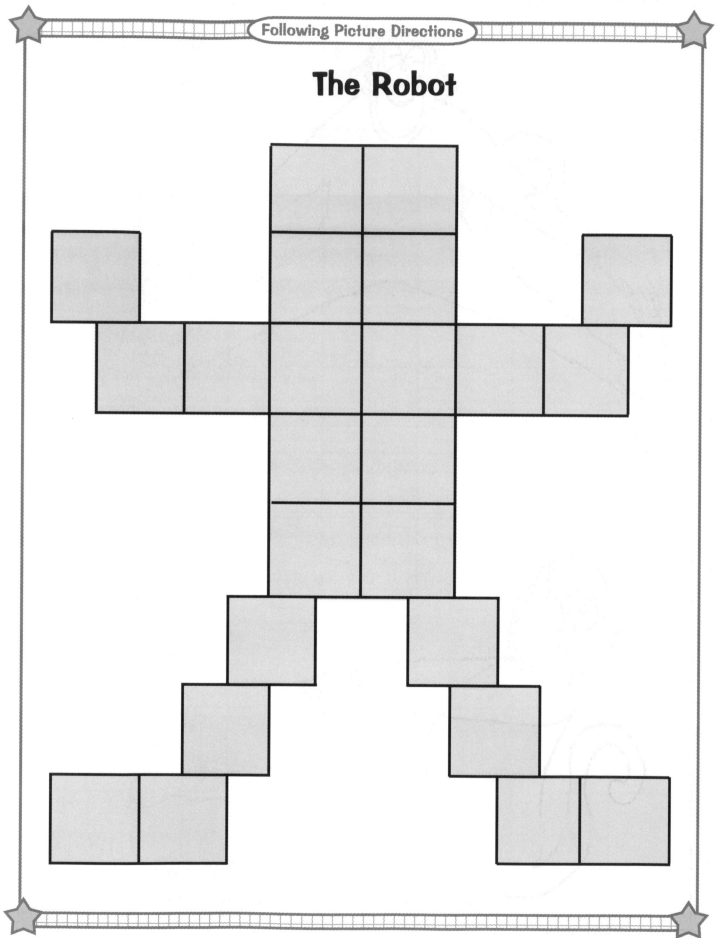

Monkey See
Monkey Do

Following Directions • EMC 738

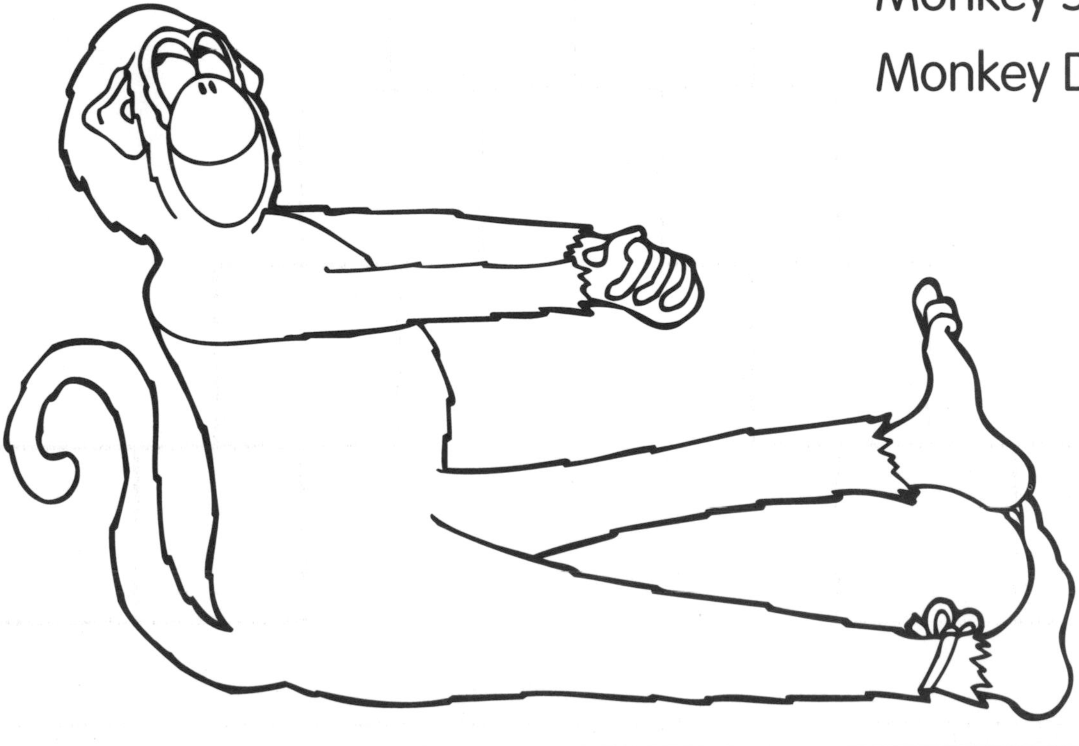

Monkey See
Monkey Do

Following Directions • EMC 738

Monkey See
Monkey Do

Monkey See
Monkey Do

Monkey See
Monkey Do

Monkey See
Monkey Do

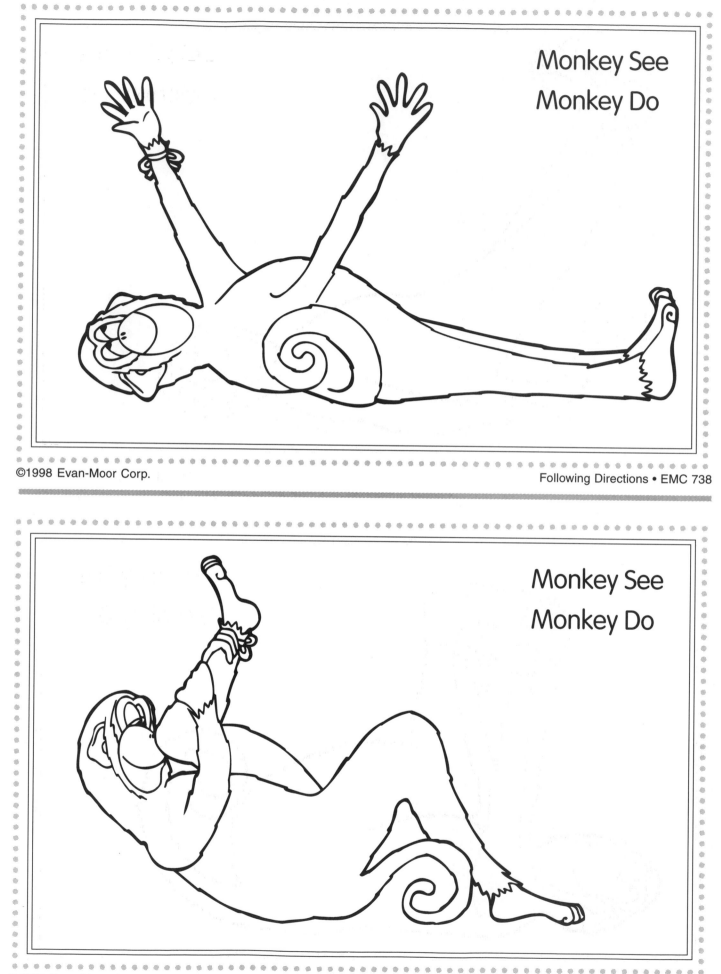

Monkey See

Monkey Do

Monkey See

Monkey Do

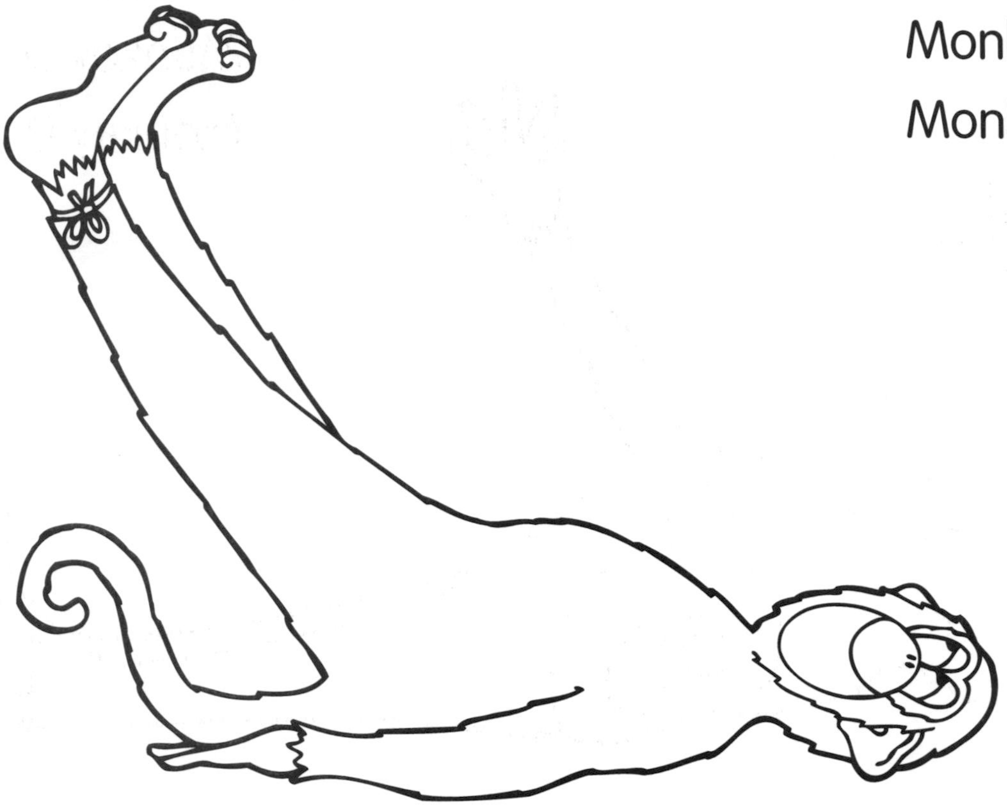

Monkey See
Monkey Do

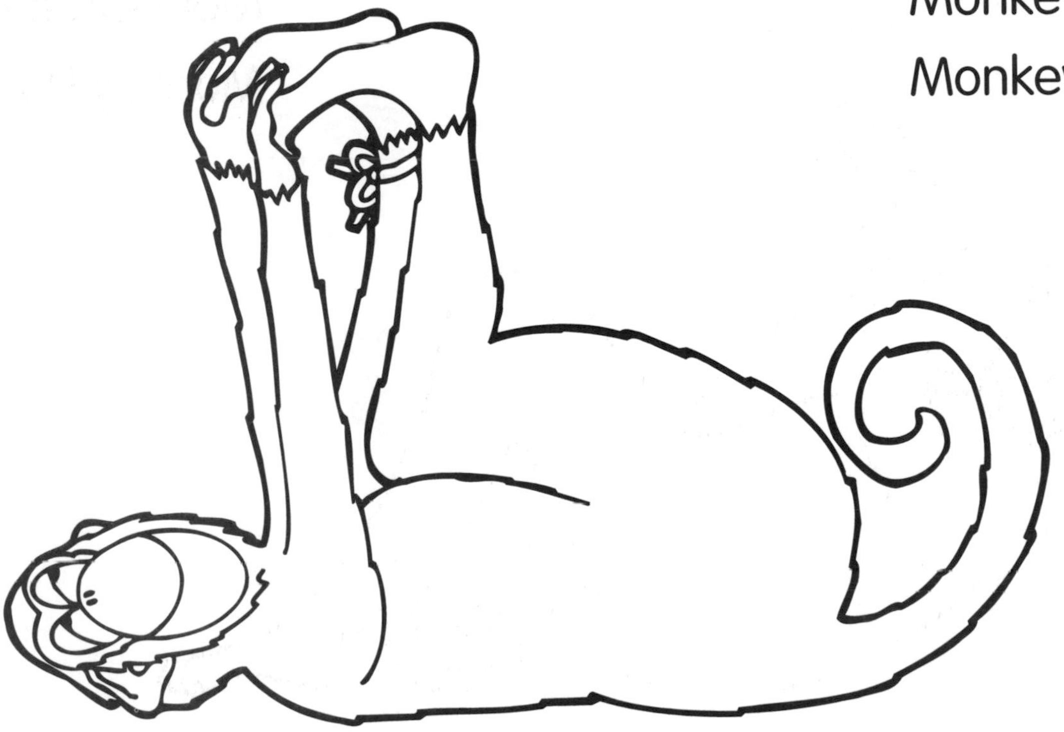

Monkey See
Monkey Do

Following Directions • EMC 738

Monkey See
Monkey Do

Monkey See
Monkey Do

Monkey See
Monkey Do

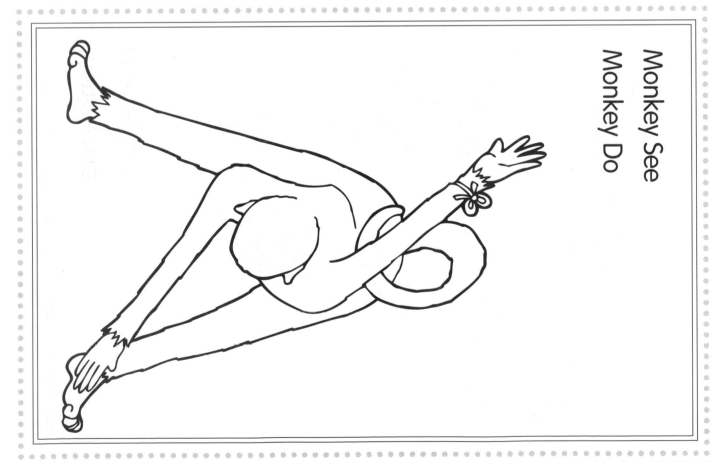

Monkey See
Monkey Do

Monkey See
Monkey Do

Following Directions • EMC 738

Monkey See
Monkey Do

Following Directions • EMC 738

Monkey See
Monkey Do

Monkey See
Monkey Do

Monkey See
Monkey Do

Following Directions • EMC 738

Monkey See
Monkey Do

Following Directions • EMC 738

Cooking with Picture Directions

Snacks are a great motivator. Young learners love to follow picture directions to make a snack for themselves. The following pages have five individual portion recipes with picture cue directions. General suggestions for setting up a cooking station are presented here with specific ingredients and utensils listed under each recipe.

Set Up a Cooking Station

1. Choose an area with a low table. Some recipes allow students to stand and move along in an assembly line manner. Other recipes, particularly those requiring cutting, will require that the students sit and use cutting boards.

2. Cover the table with a heavy plastic or oil cloth cover to facilitate easy clean-up. Set out the utensils and ingredients for each step along with a laminated copy of the picture directions. Clothespin the picture directions to a sturdy bookend for easy reading.

3. Discuss and demonstrate proper techniques for following the directions as needed. Have students move through the steps independently. Any time young learners are using any cooking imlements, it is imperative to remain alert and watchful.

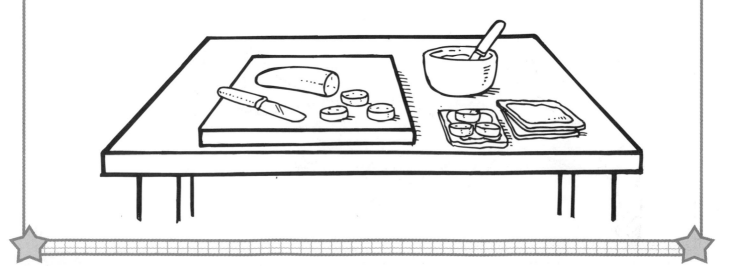

What You Will Need:

▶ Graham Goodies ———————————————————
(for each serving)

      1 graham cracker
      1 tablespoon of frosting
      plastic knife or spreader

▶ Peanut Butter Banana Cracker ———————————————————
(for each serving)

      1 soda cracker
      1 teaspoon peanut butter honey mixture (1/2 cup peanut butter mixed
         with 1/4 cup honey)
      1/4 peeled banana
      Plastic knife or spreader
      Cutting board

▶ Grape Dippers ———————————————————
(for each serving)

      2 tablespoons honey yogurt mixture (1 cup vanilla yogurt + 2 tablespoons
         of honey)
      8 grapes
      Small cup or bowl
      Toothpick or plastic fork
      Tablespoon for measuring

▶ Lettuce Roll-ups ———————————————————
(for each serving)

      1 leaf of lettuce
      1 tablespoon of peanut butter honey paint (½ cup of peanut butter mixed
         with ½ cup of honey)
      Pastry brush

▶ Sunshine Sipper ———————————————————
(for each serving)

      ½ cup of orange juice
      1 teaspoon of powdered milk
      2 ice cubes
      ½ cup measuring cup
      Glass
      Blender

Graham Goodies

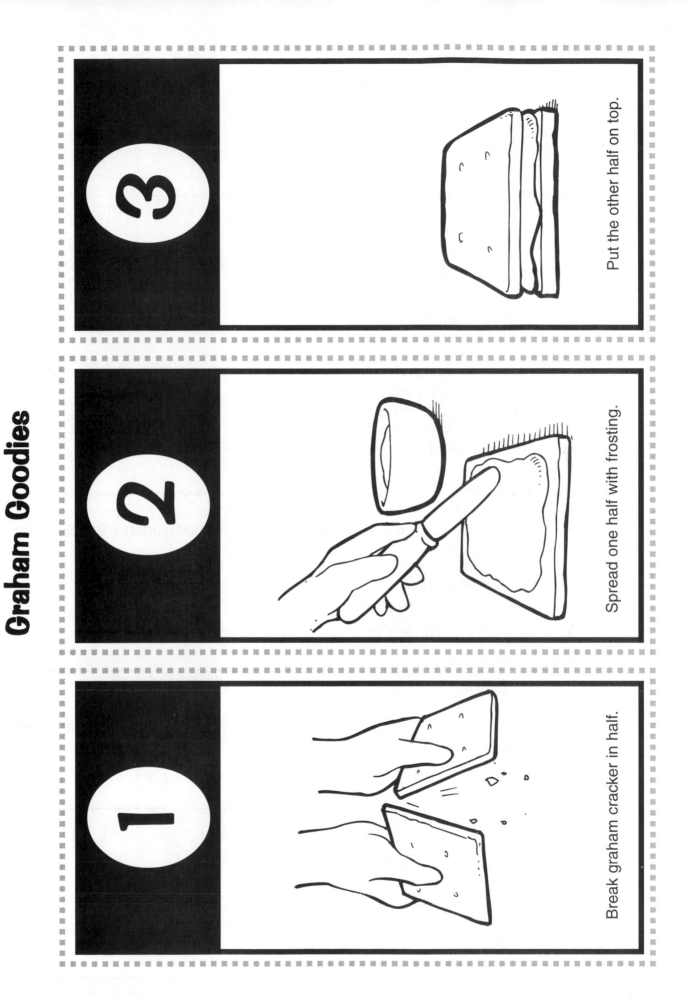

1 Break graham cracker in half.

2 Spread one half with frosting.

3 Put the other half on top.

Peanut Butter Banana Crackers

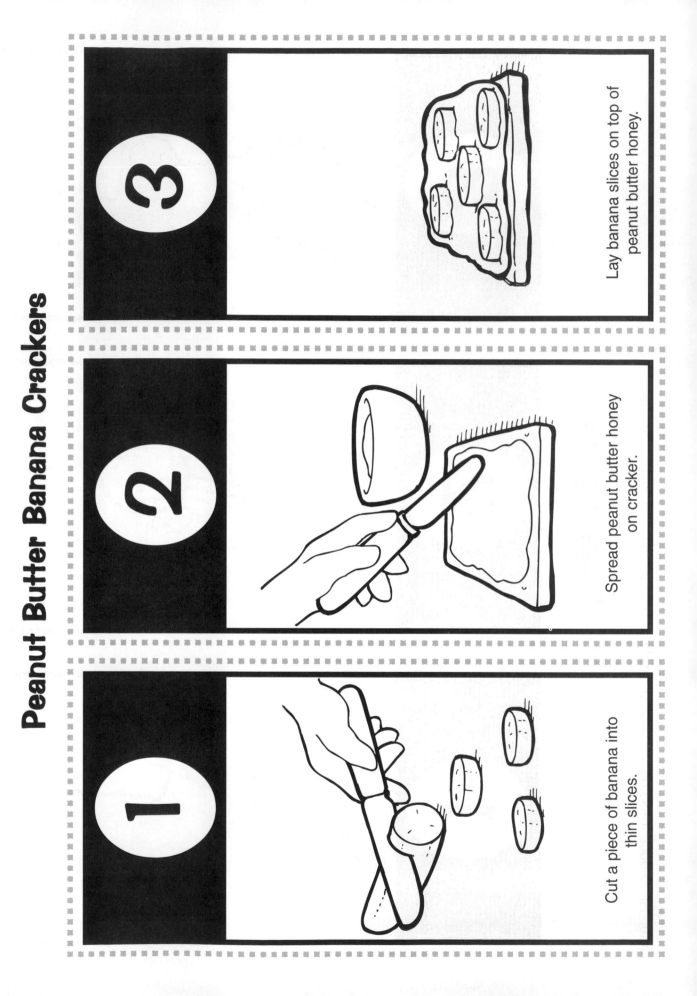

3 Lay banana slices on top of peanut butter honey.

2 Spread peanut butter honey on cracker.

1 Cut a piece of banana into thin slices.

Note: Reproduce these direction cards and laminate them to use when cooking.

Grape Dippers

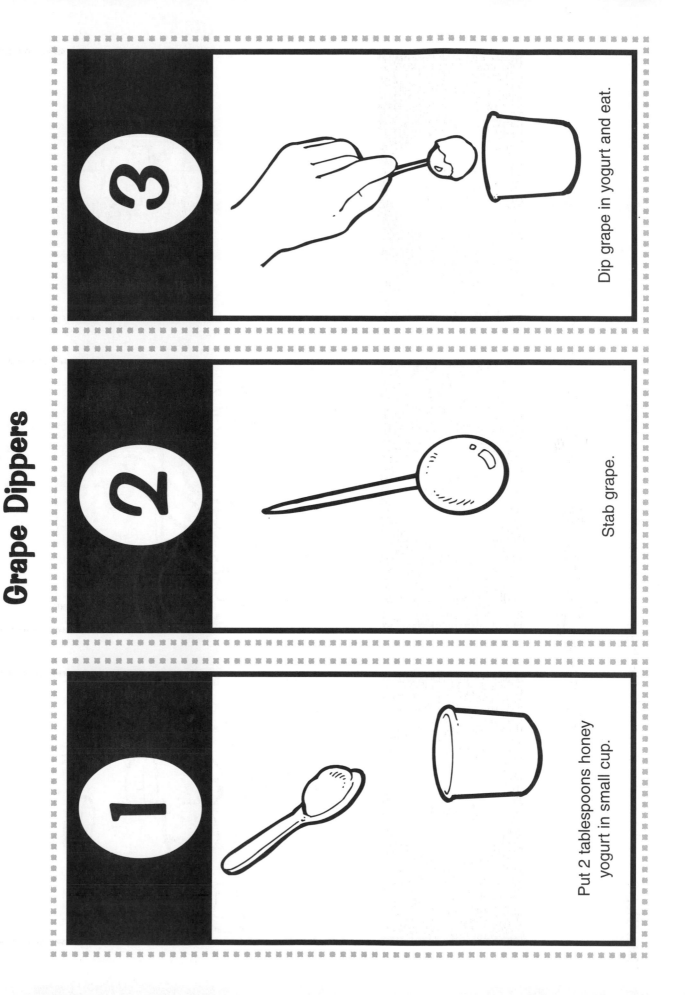

3 — Dip grape in yogurt and eat.

2 — Stab grape.

1 — Put 2 tablespoons honey yogurt in small cup.

Note: Reproduce these direction cards and laminate them to use when cooking.

Lettuce Roll-ups

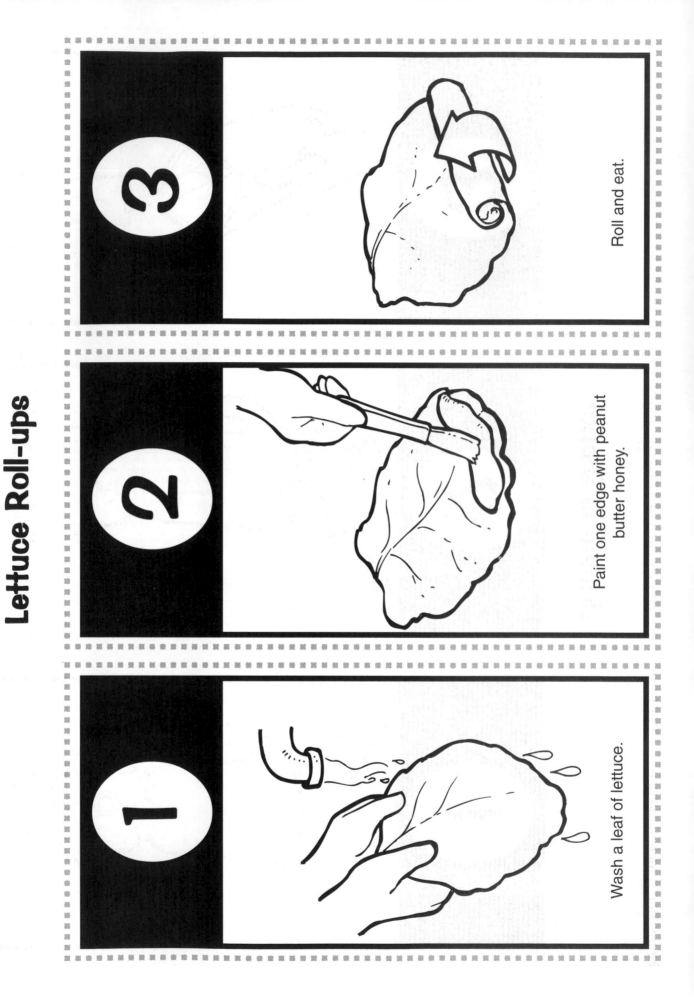

3 Roll and eat.

2 Paint one edge with peanut butter honey.

1 Wash a leaf of lettuce.

Note: Reproduce these direction cards and laminate them to use when cooking.

Sunshine Sipper

3

Blend and drink.

2

Add 1 teaspoon powdered milk and 2 ice cubes.

1

Pour ½ cup of orange juice into blender.

Teacher Directions for Student Worksheets

Trace and Make

Pages 65-68

Materials:

• worksheet

• crayons

Directions:

1. Go over the picture directions at the top of each worksheet.

2. Remind students to keep referring back to the directions as they complete each section of the worksheet.

Match the Shapes

Pages 69-70

Materials:

• worksheet

• pattern blocks or pattern cut-outs on page 112.

Directions:

1. You may want to laminate these pages so that they cn be reused.

2. Tell students that they are going to cover the picture using pattern blocks (or pattern cut-outs) that exactly match the shapes in the picture.

3. For a more challenging activity, instruct students to use pattern blocks to duplicate the picture beside the original.

Name: _____

Trace and Make

1.

2.

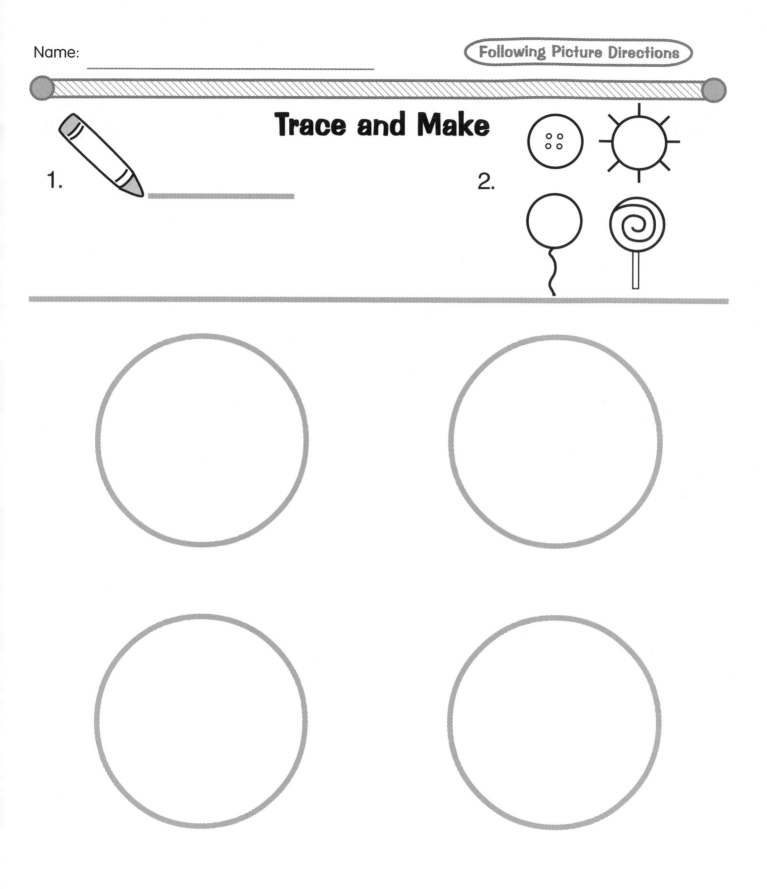

Name: _____

Trace and Make

1. _____

2.

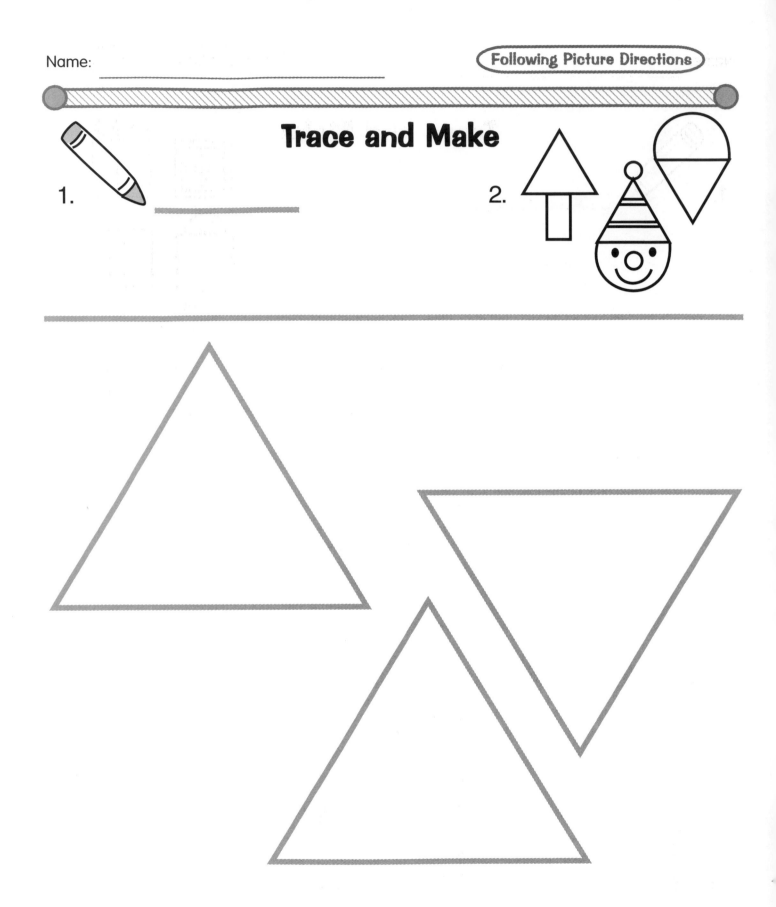

Name: _____

Trace and Make

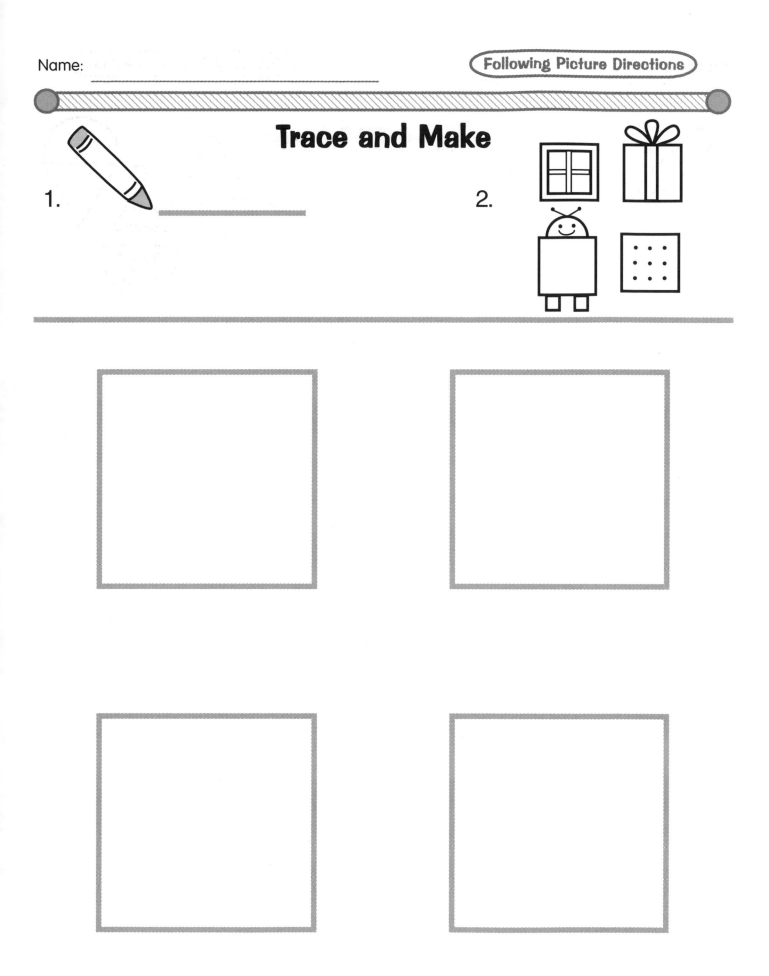

1.

2.

Name: _____

Trace and Make

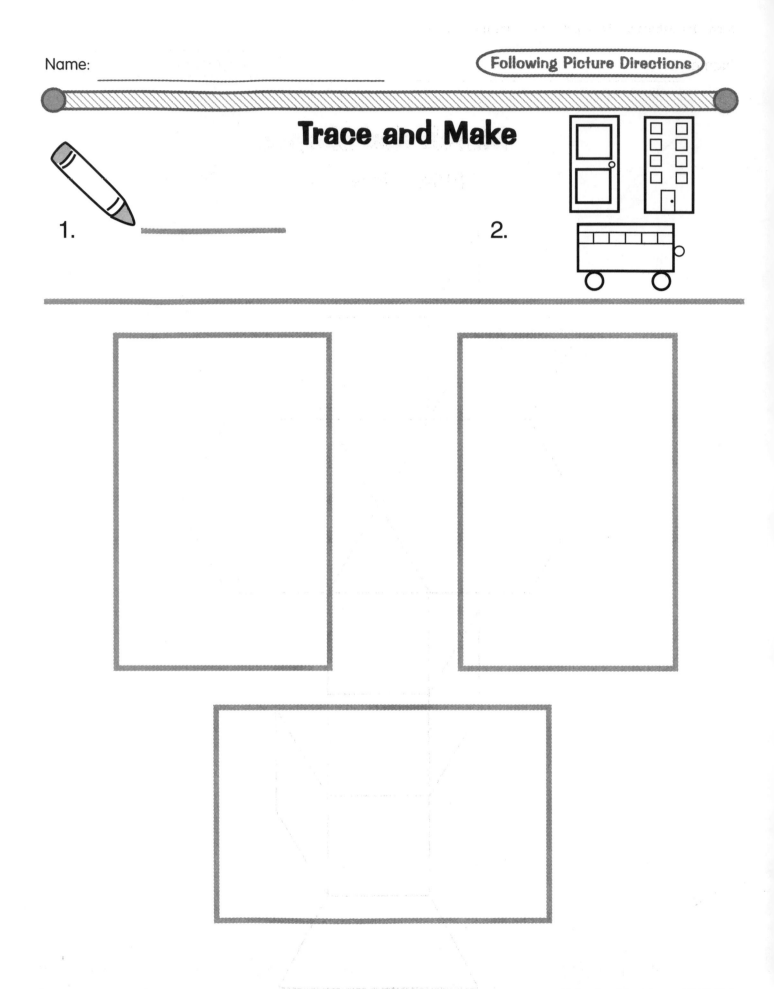

1.

2.

Name: _____

Match the Shapes

Flower in a Pot

Name: _____

Match the Shapes

Duckie Duddle

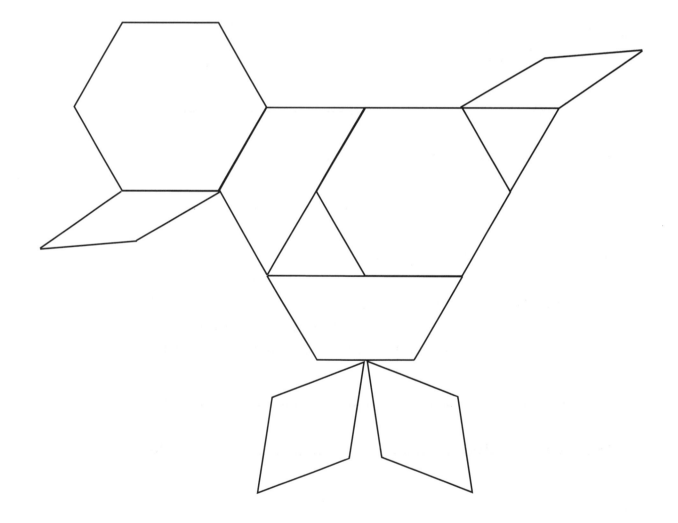

Following Written Directions

As your students begin recognizing words and using context to bring meaning to those words, use written cues to give directions. The following activity pages use pictures and words or simple words alone for the directions.

Students need crayons for all the activities in this section; scissors and paste for some of the activities. Cut and paste activities require additional paper.

Included in this section:

For these pages provide 1" colored blocks or 1" (2.5 cm) squares of colored paper for students to use in duplicating the designs.

Name: _____

Color the Shapes

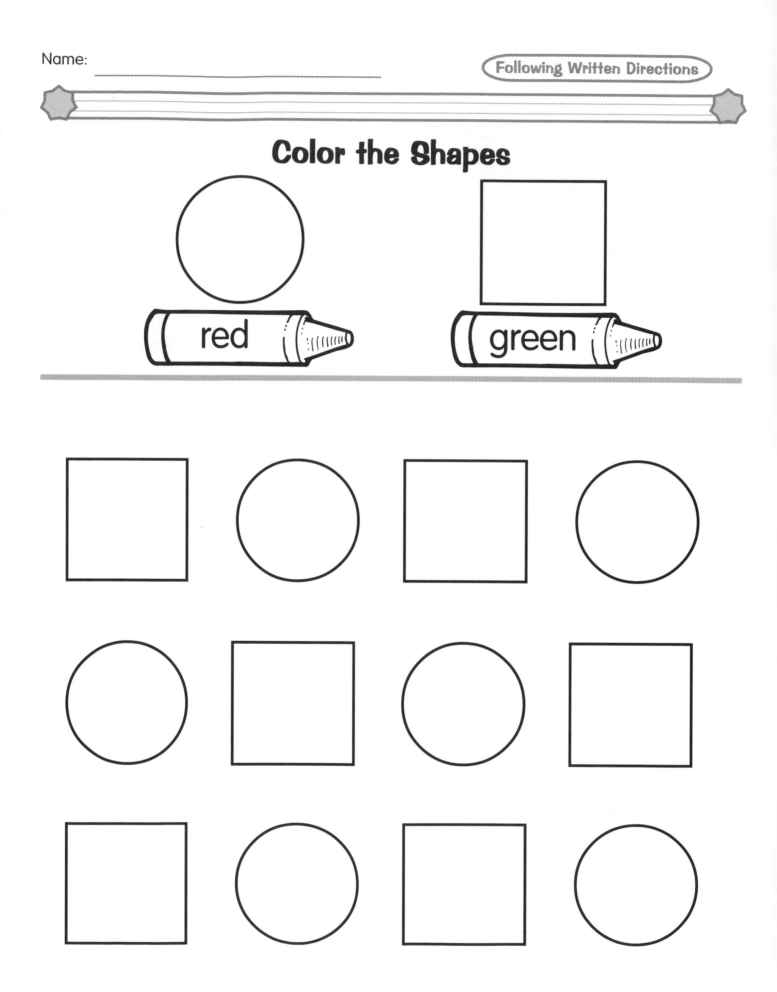

Following Directions • EMC 738

Name: _____

Color the Shapes

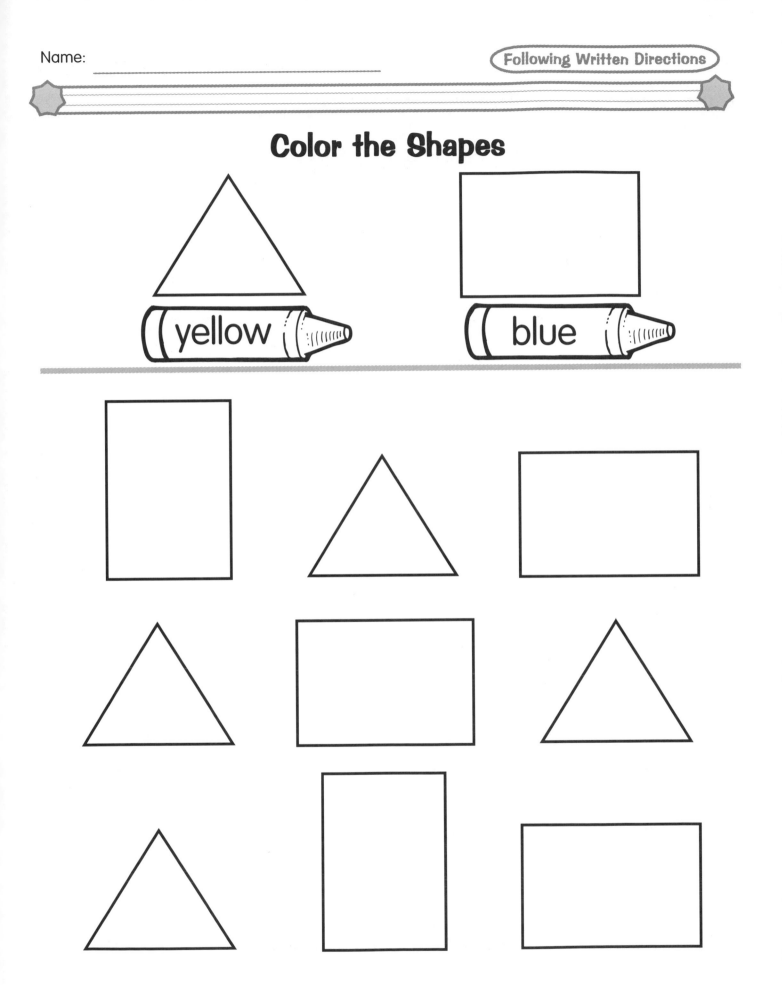

yellow

blue

Following Directions • EMC 738

Name: _____

Color the Shapes

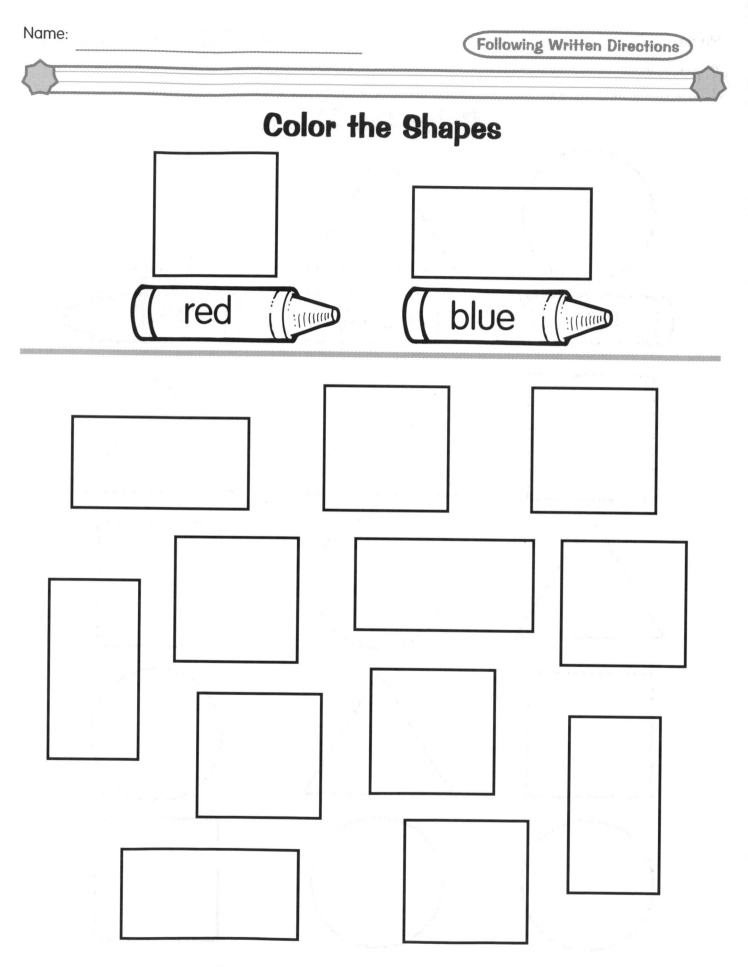

Name: _____

Color the Shapes

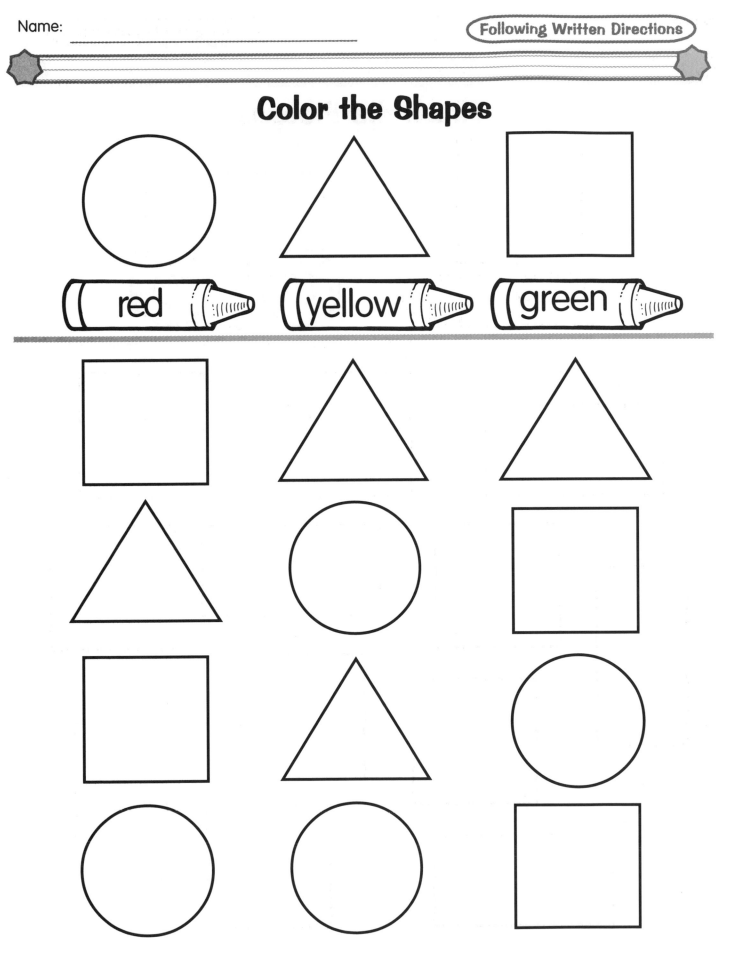

Finish the Picture

wagon

Color the wagon red.

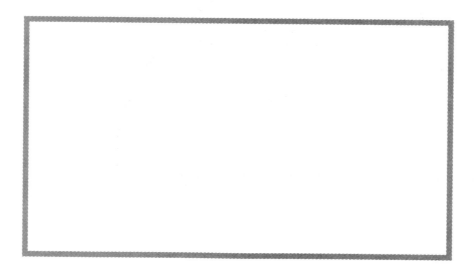

Finish the Picture

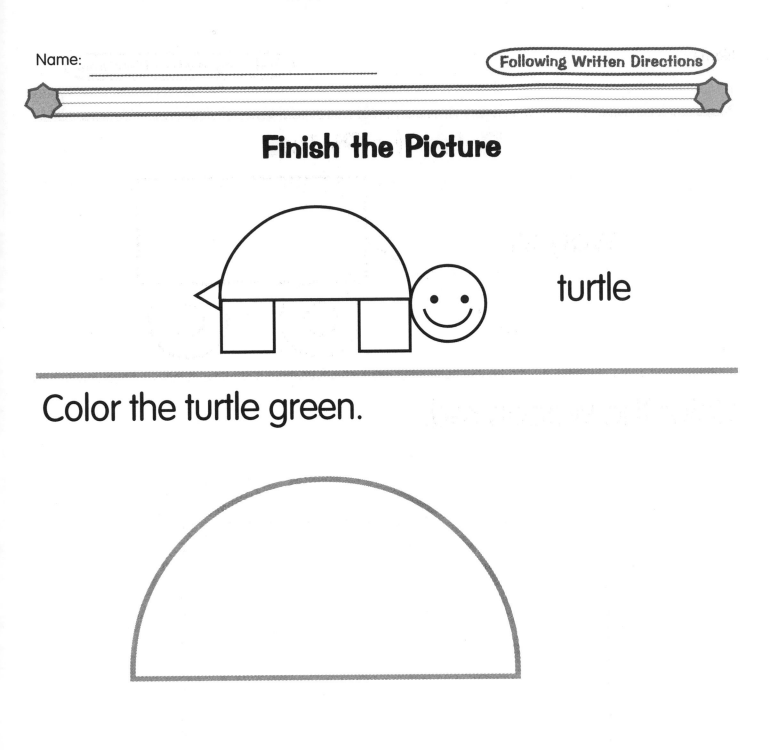

turtle

Color the turtle green.

Finish the Picture

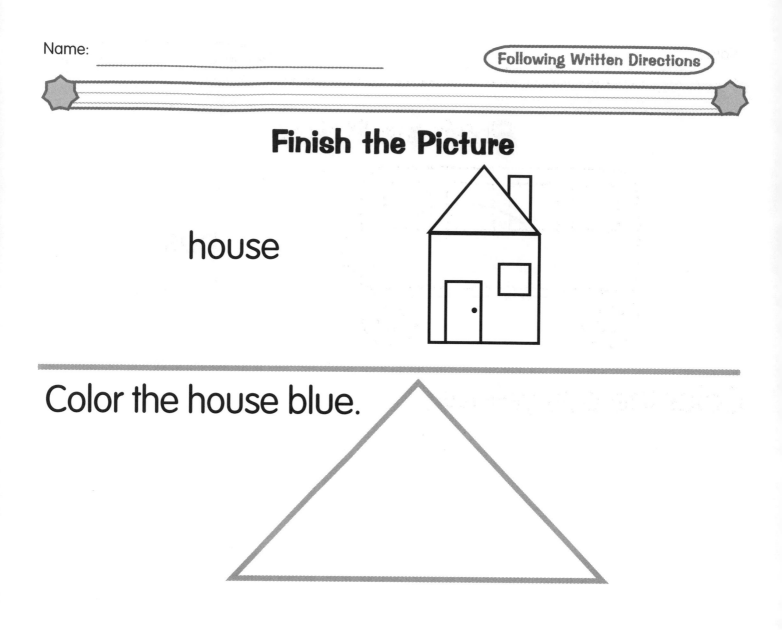

house

Color the house blue.

Finish the Picture

bus

Color the bus yellow.

Find the Shapes and Color

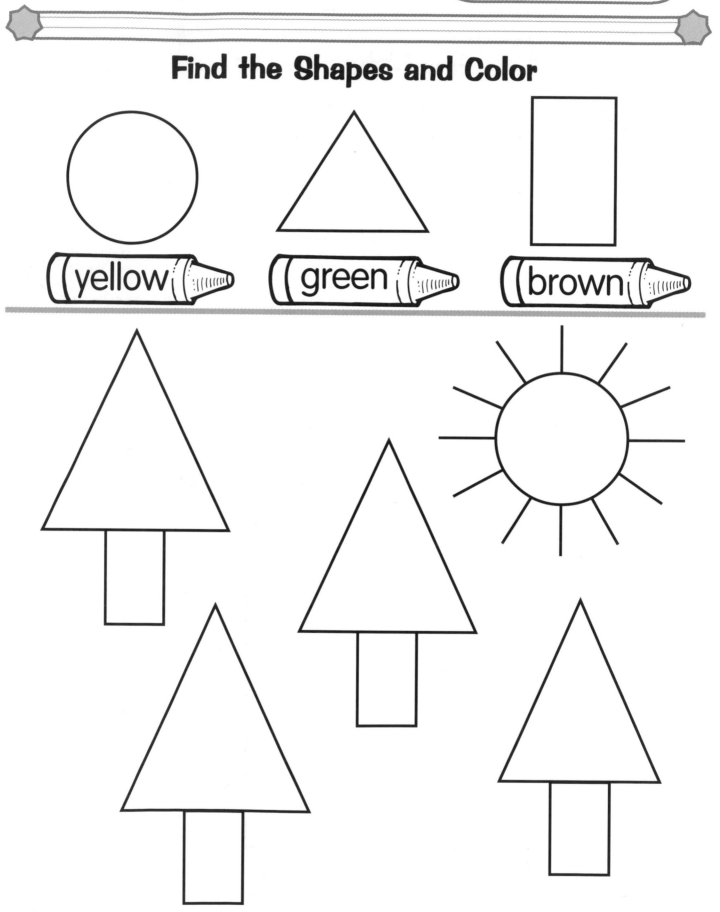

yellow

green

brown

Find the Shapes and Color

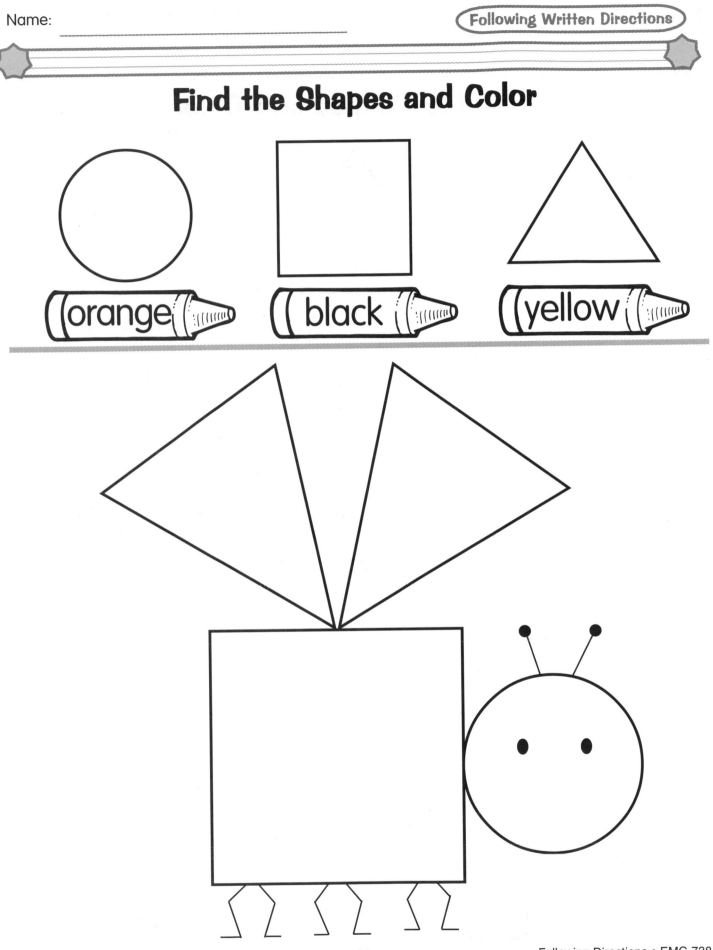

Name: _____

Find the Shapes and Color

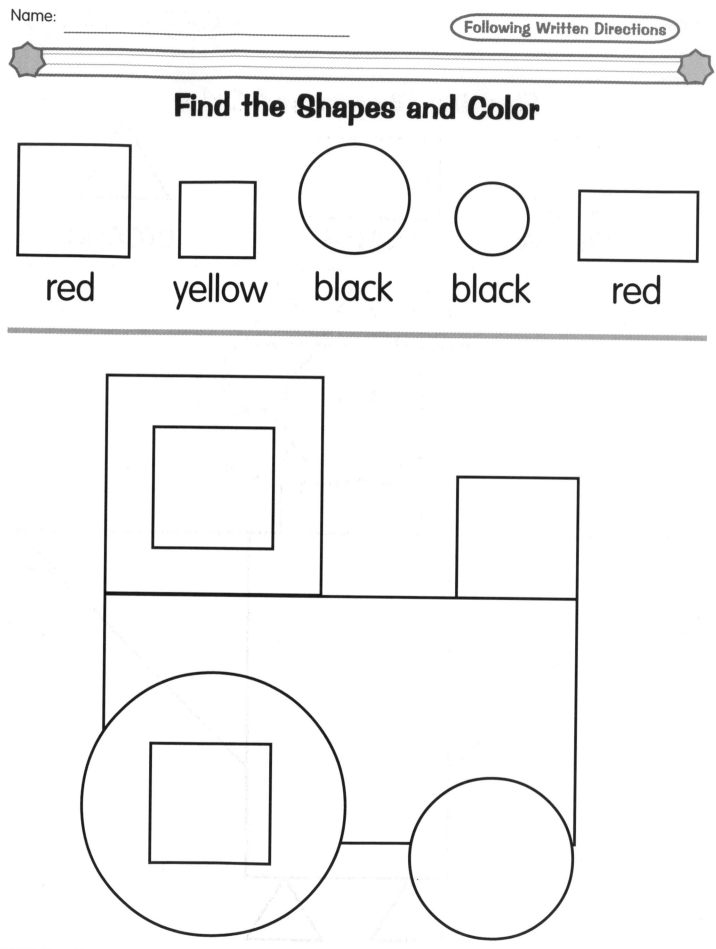

red   yellow   black   black   red

Find the Shapes and Color

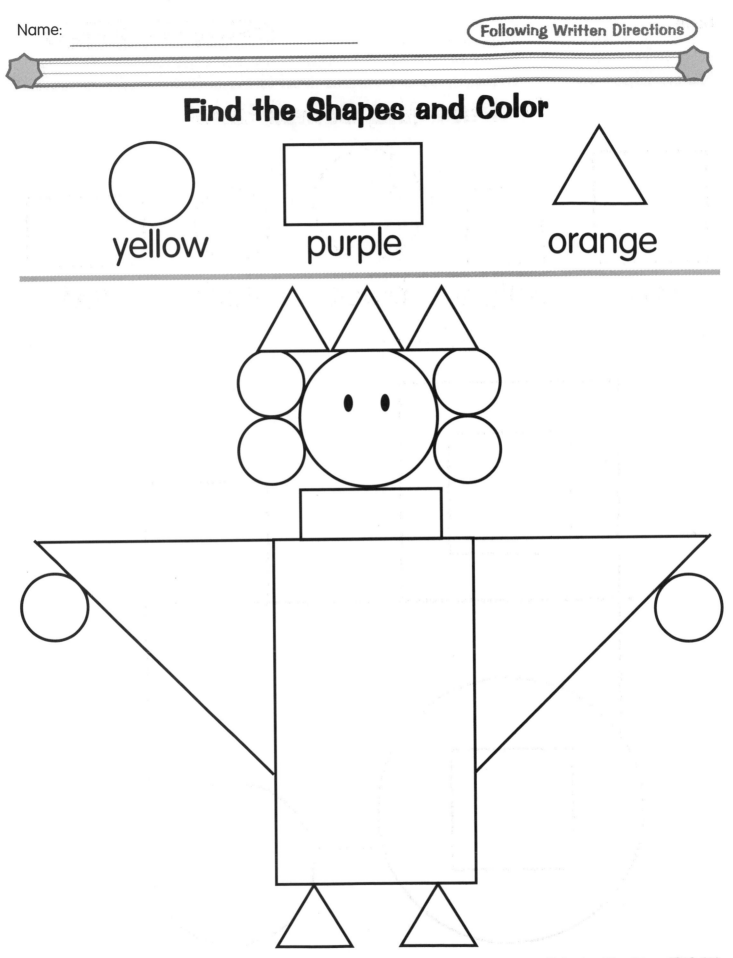

yellow   purple   orange

Name: _____

Trace and Complete

1. Trace

_____

2. Add

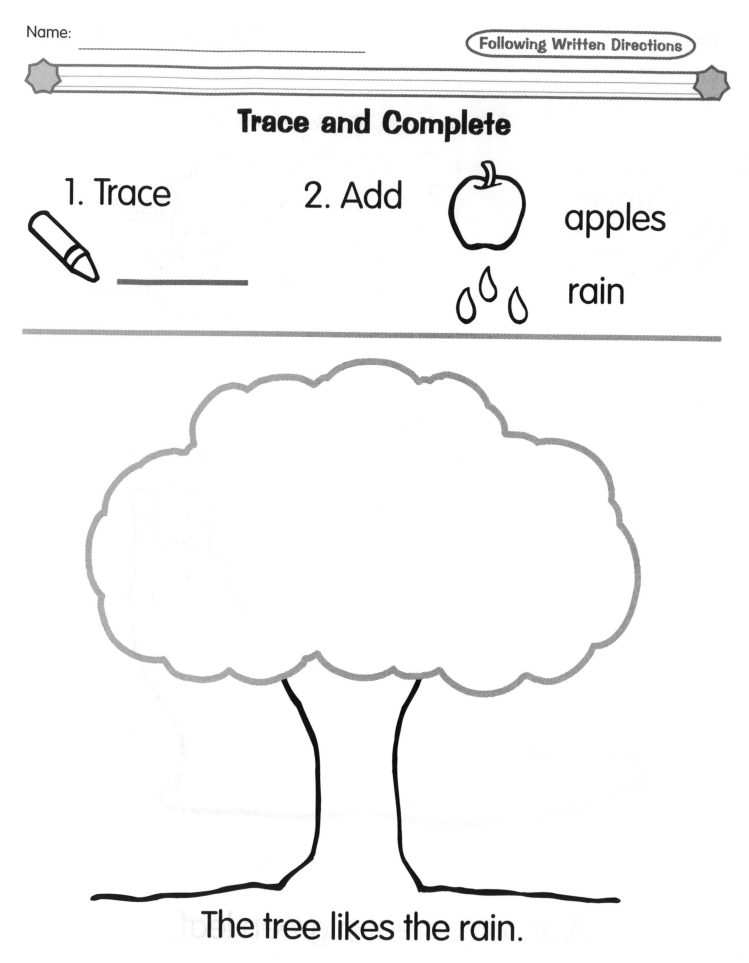

apples

rain

The tree likes the rain.

Trace and Complete

1. Trace _____

2. Add

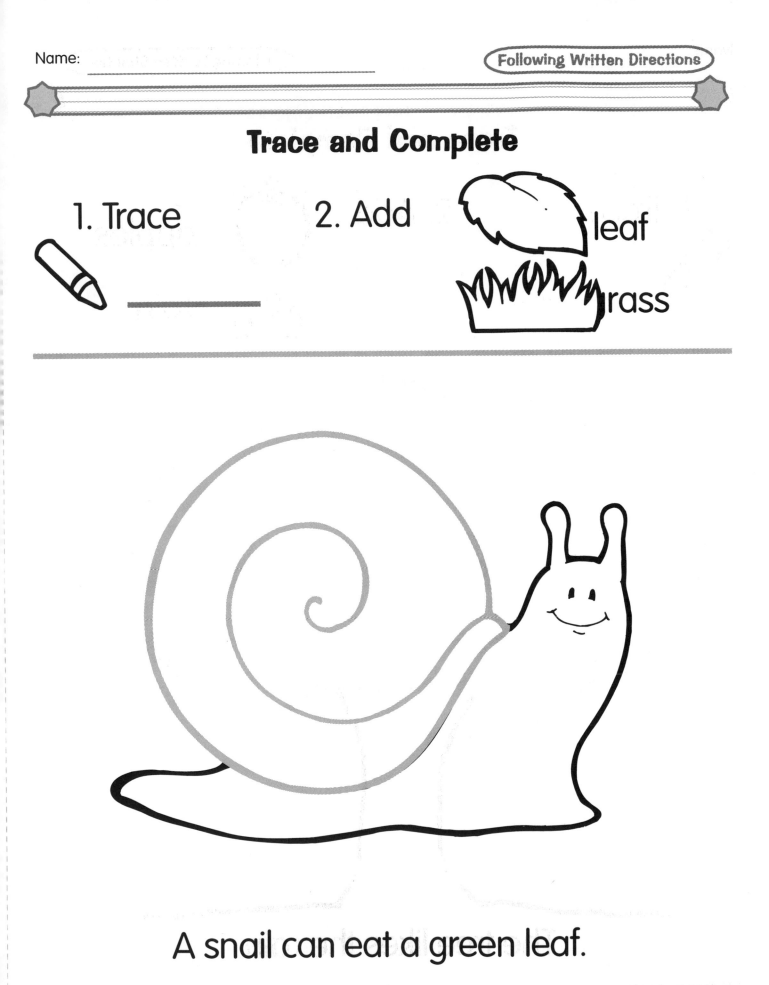

leaf

rass

A snail can eat a green leaf.

Name: _____

Trace and Complete

1. Trace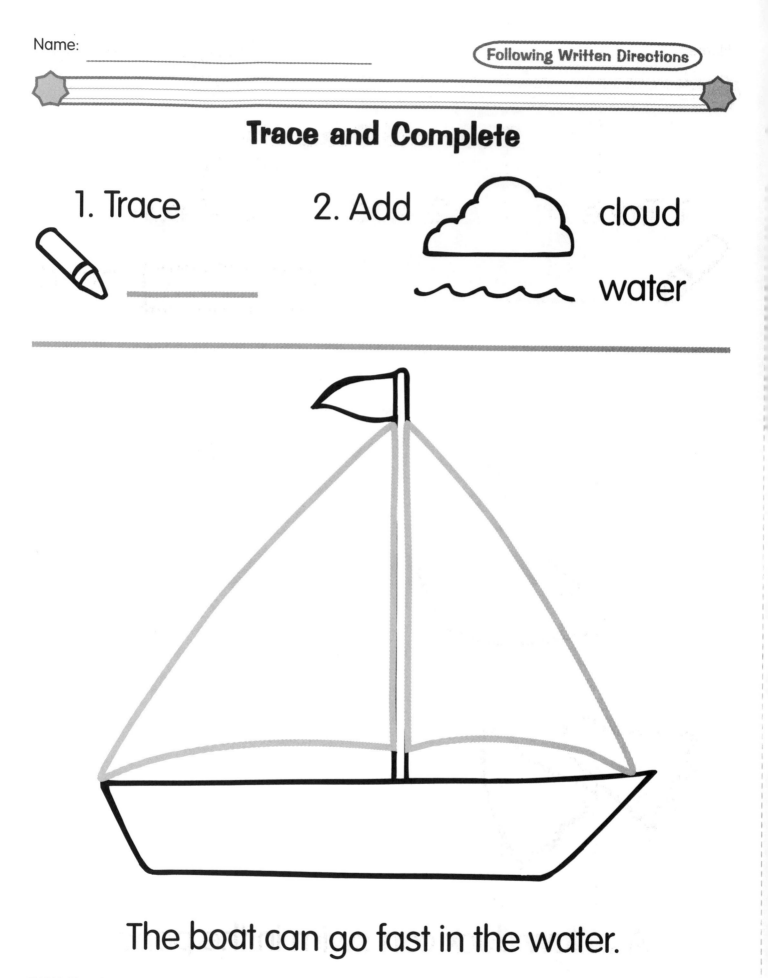

_____

2. Add cloud

water

The boat can go fast in the water.

Name: _____

Trace and Complete

1. Trace

2. Add ◯ sun

🖍 _____

〰️ pond

A yellow duck can swim in the pond.

Name: _____

Color, Cut, and Paste

1. 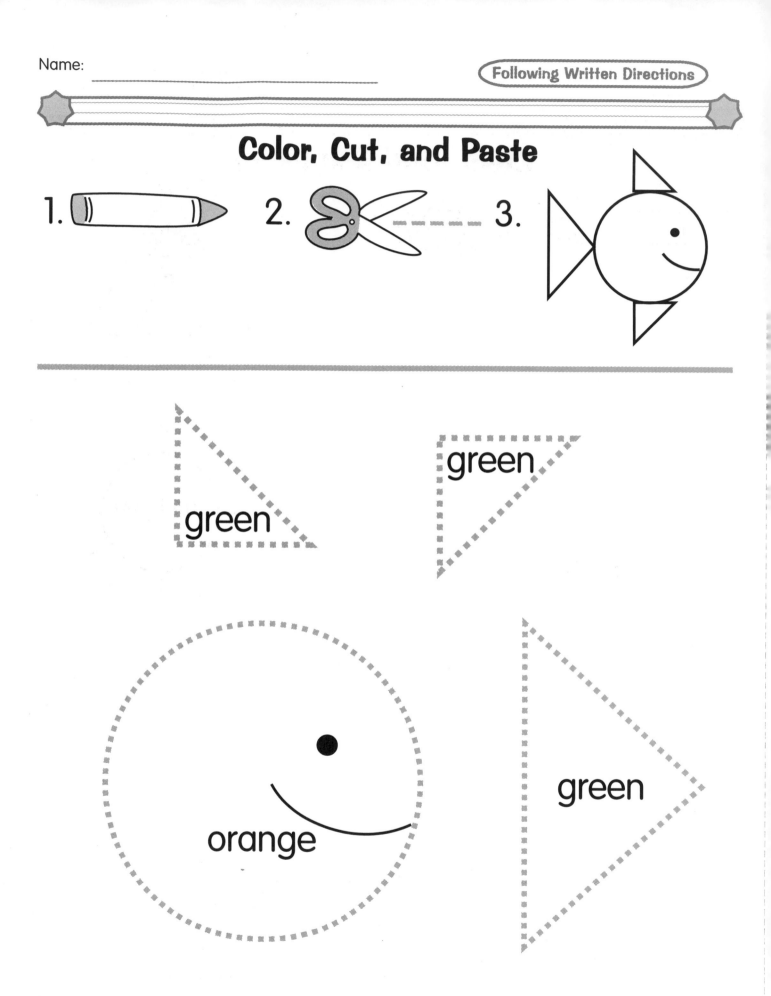   2.   - - - - -   3.

green

green

orange

green

Name: _____

Color, Cut, and Paste

1. 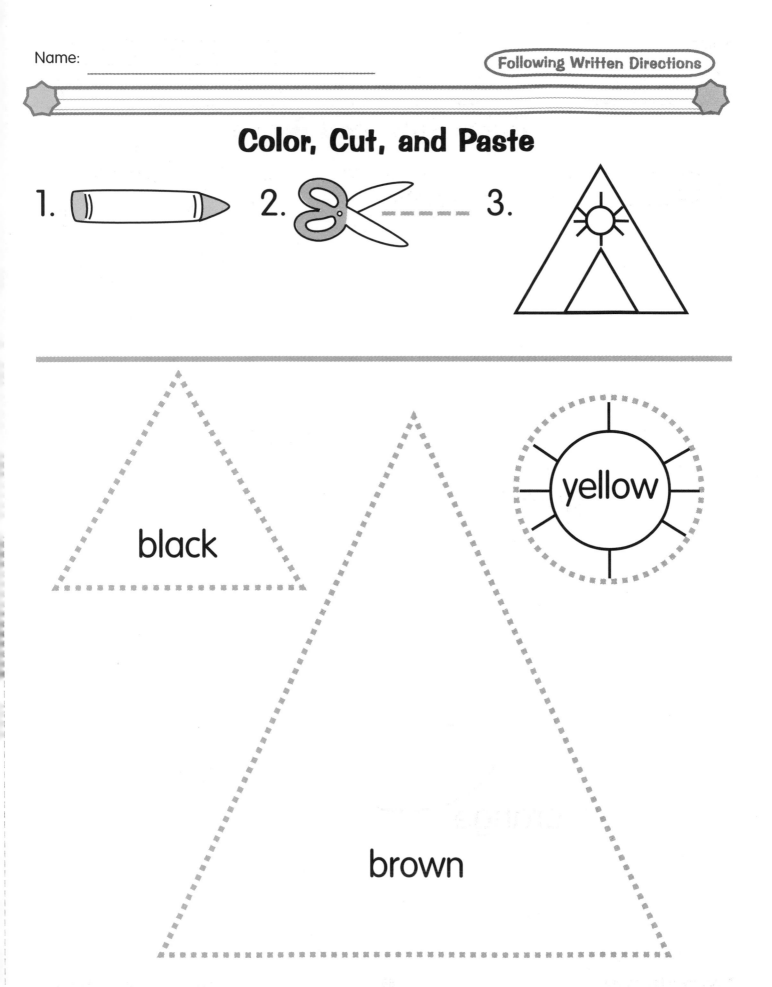 2. - - - - - 3.

---

black

brown

yellow

Name: _____

Color, Cut, and Paste

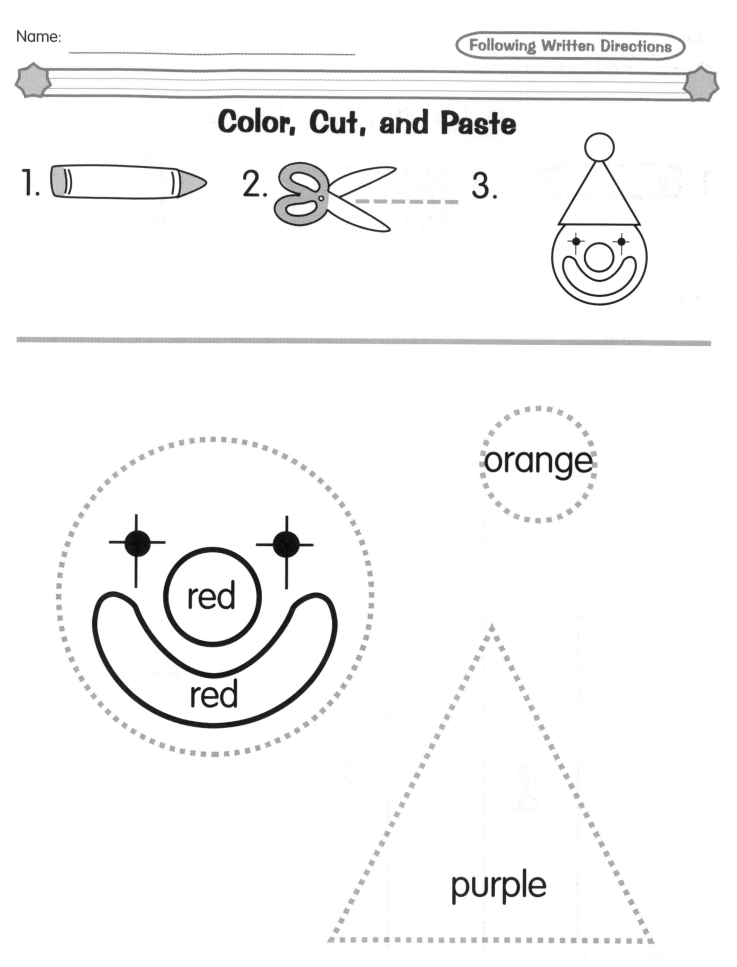

1. 2. 3.

orange

red

red

purple

Name: _____

Color, Cut, and Paste

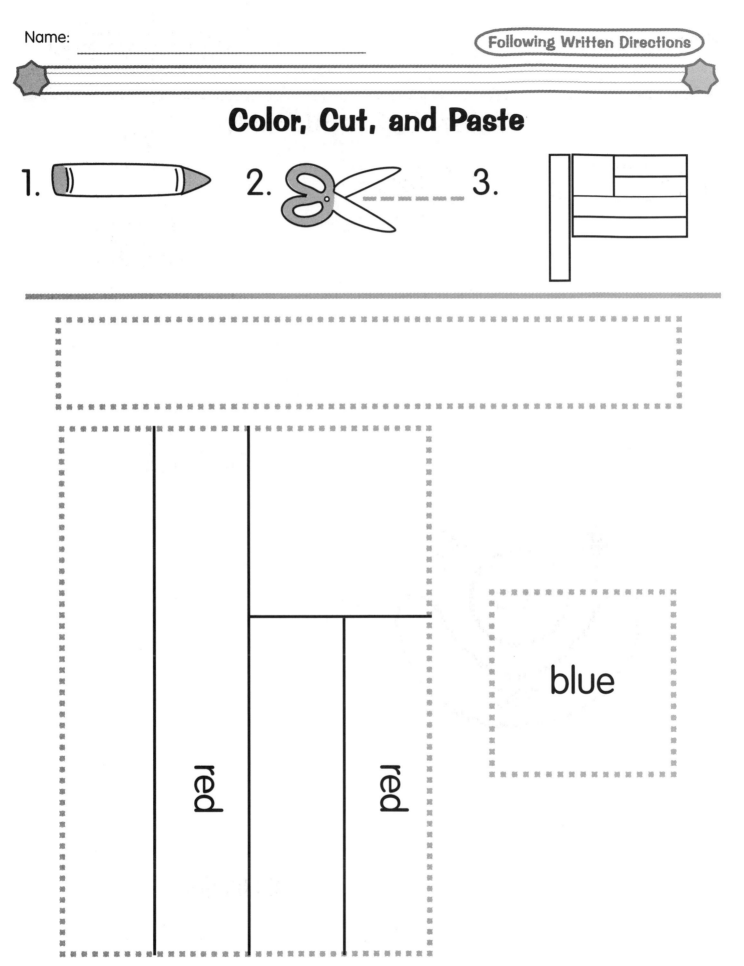

1. 2. 3.

red

red

blue

Name: _____

Read and Match Colors

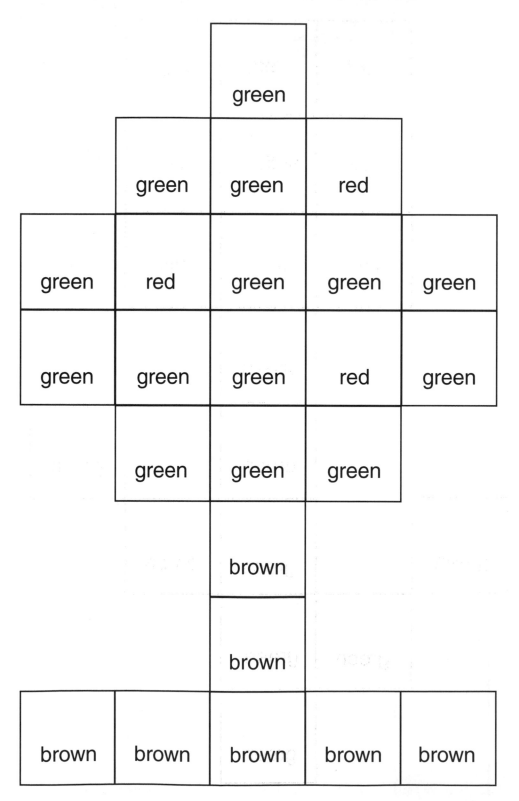

Read and Match Colors

red	red	red
red	yellow	red
red	red	red

	green	
	green	green
green	green	green
green	green	
	green	

Name: _____

Draw It

Make a red, blue, and yellow

I see a red, blue, and yellow house.

Draw It

Make a brown

I see a brown mouse.

Name: _____

Draw It

Make a green

I see a green caterpillar.

Draw It

Make 2 blue

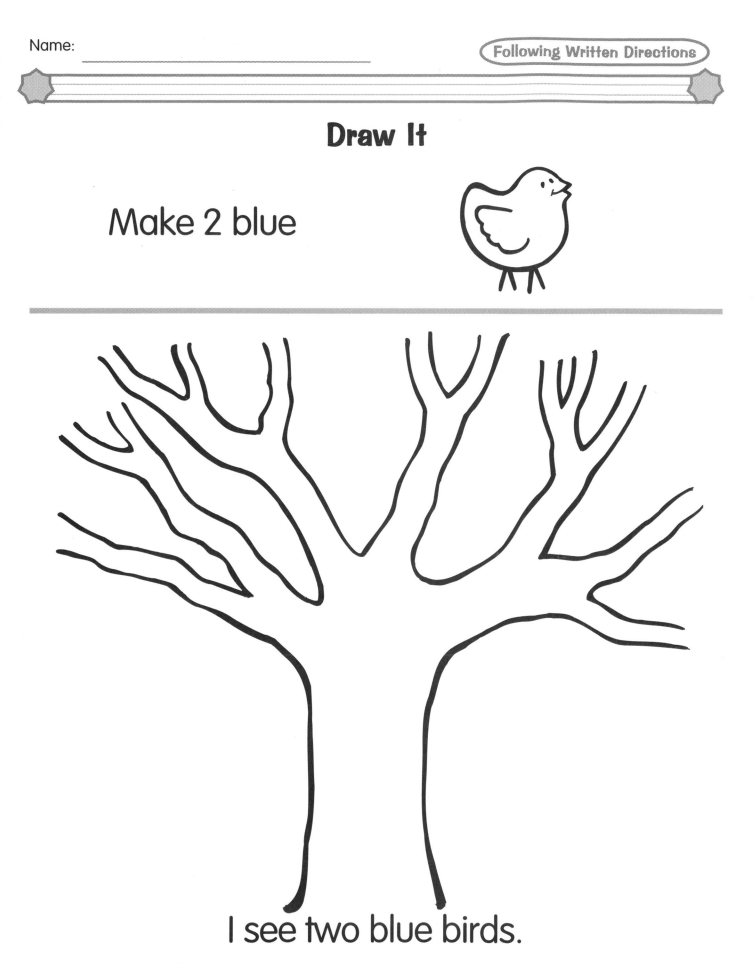

I see two blue birds.

Cut, Paste, and Add

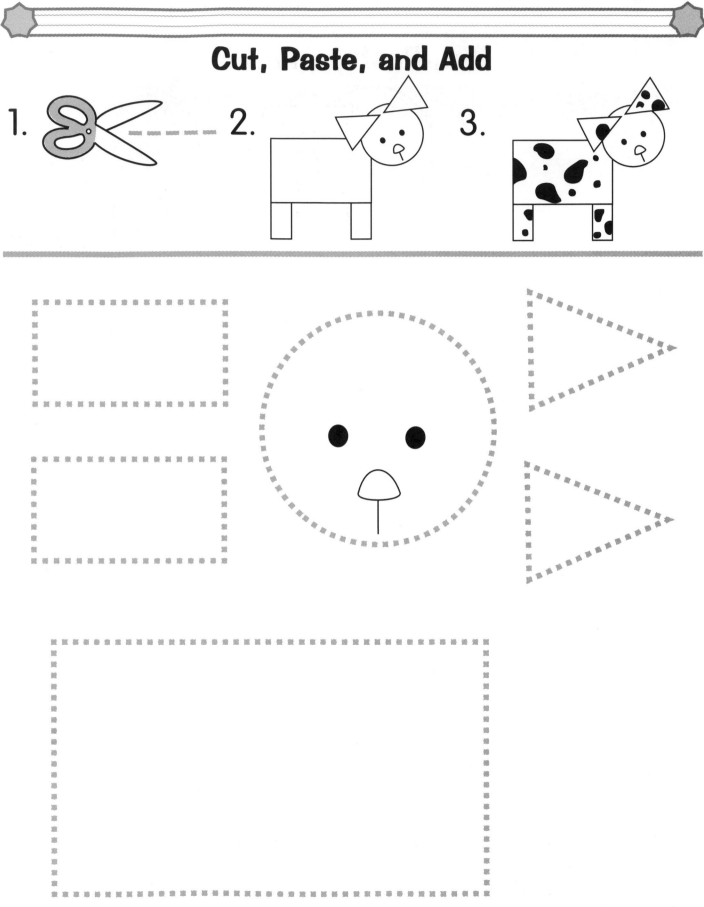

Cut, Paste, and Add

Cut, Paste, and Add

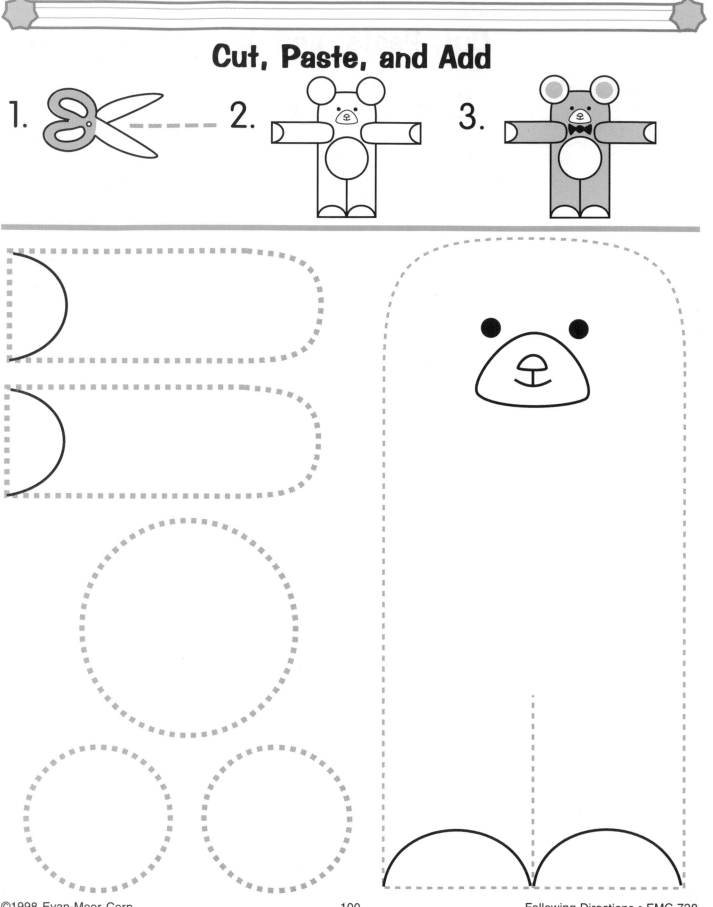

1. 2. 3.

Cut, Paste, and Add

1. 2. 3.

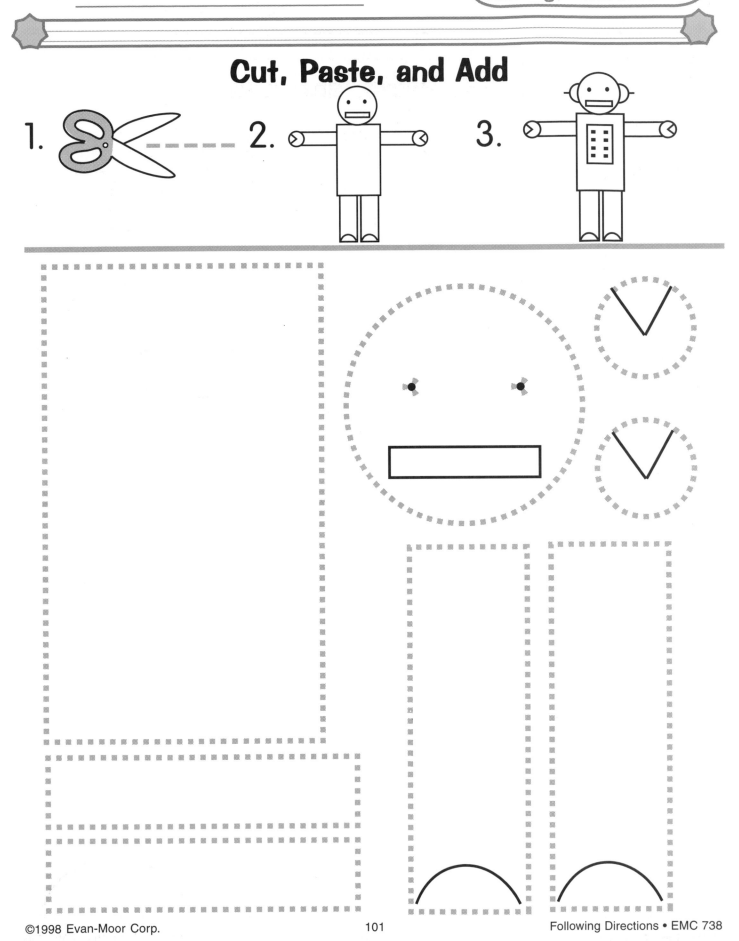

Name: _____

Categories

Color things to eat yellow.

Color things to ride blue.

Color things to wear red.

Color things to sit on green.

Name: _____

Categories

List your 10 favorite foods:

1. _____   6. _____

2. _____   7. _____

3. _____   8. _____

4. _____   9. _____

5. _____   10. _____

Now: (vegetables)   ~~meat~~   [fruit]   all other foods

Draw your most favorite food here.

Categories

Color

number names	**purple**
color words	**red**
boy names	**black**
girl names	**yellow**

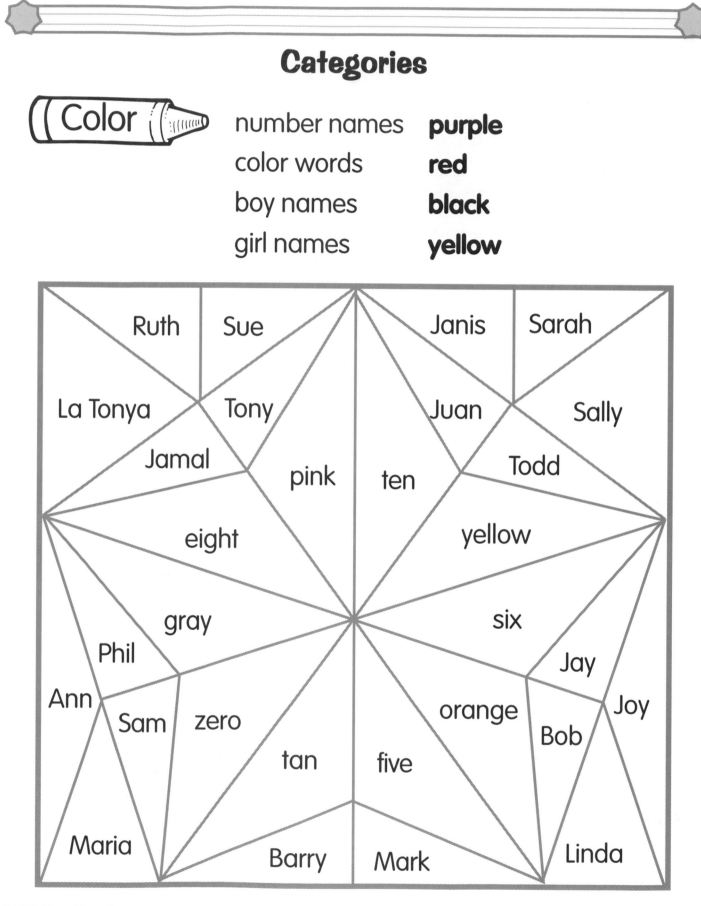

Ruth   Sue   Janis   Sarah

La Tonya   Tony   Juan   Sally

Jamal   Todd

pink   ten   yellow

eight

gray   six

Phil   Jay

Ann   orange   Joy

Sam   zero   Bob

tan   five

Maria   Barry   Mark   Linda

Make It

Follow the directions to make a mask.

1. Get a 9" x 12" sheet of colored paper.

2. Cut:

save for ears

3. Curl the hair.
   Paste the ears on.

4. Get scraps of paper.
   Cut out eyes and a nose.
   Draw a mouth. Color the face.

examples:

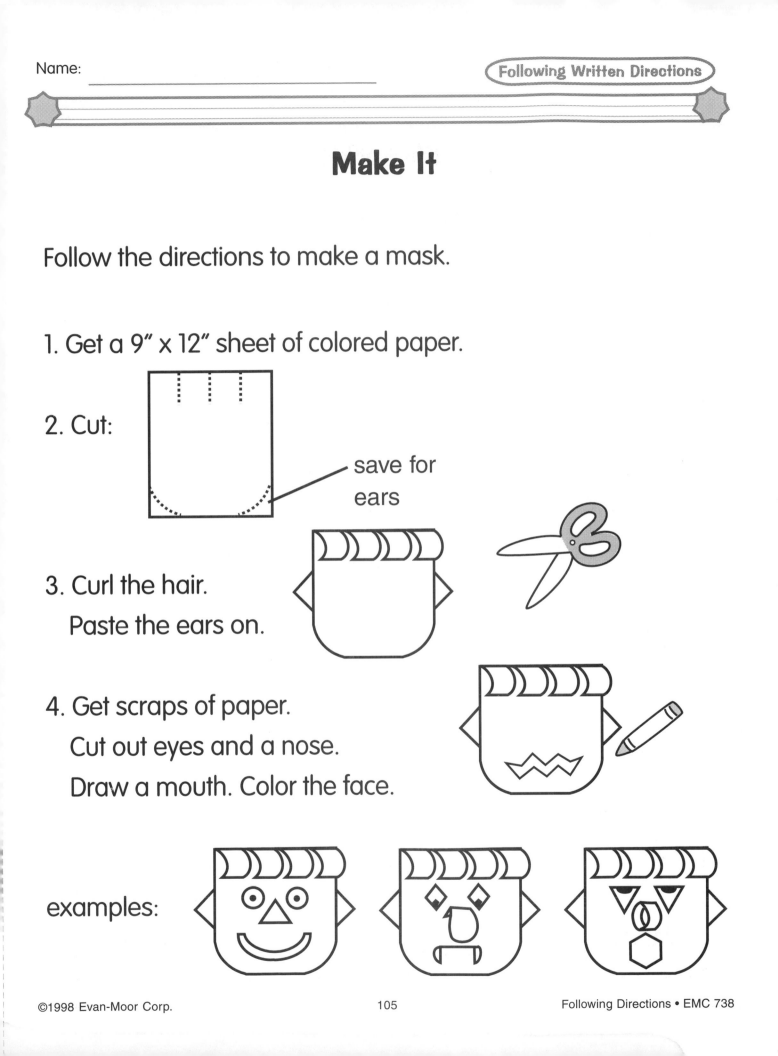

Make It

1. Cut out the rectangle.

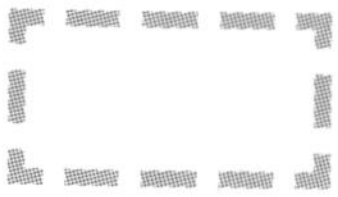

2. Fold in half on the _____ line.

3. Cut all the ||| lines.

4. Open the paper.

5. Paste the ends together.

6. Add a string handle.

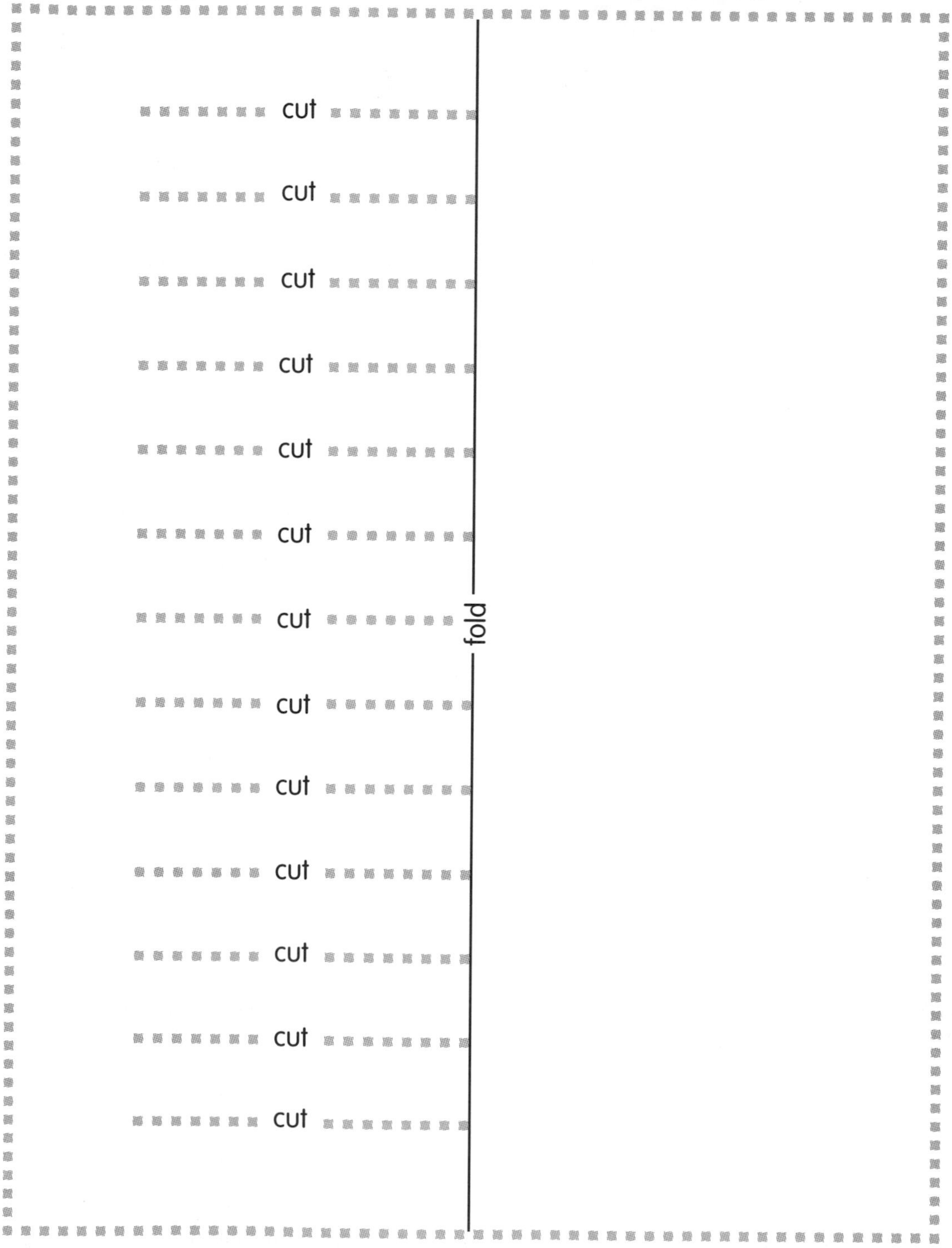

cut

cut

cut

cut

cut

cut

cut

cut

cut

cut

cut

cut

cut

fold

Make It

Color each box to make a picture.

16	11	3	12	9	7
Blue with a purple fish	red	white / yellow	red / white	red / white	yellow with an orange sun

15	10	13	8	2	14
blue	red	blue	white / yellow	white green	blue

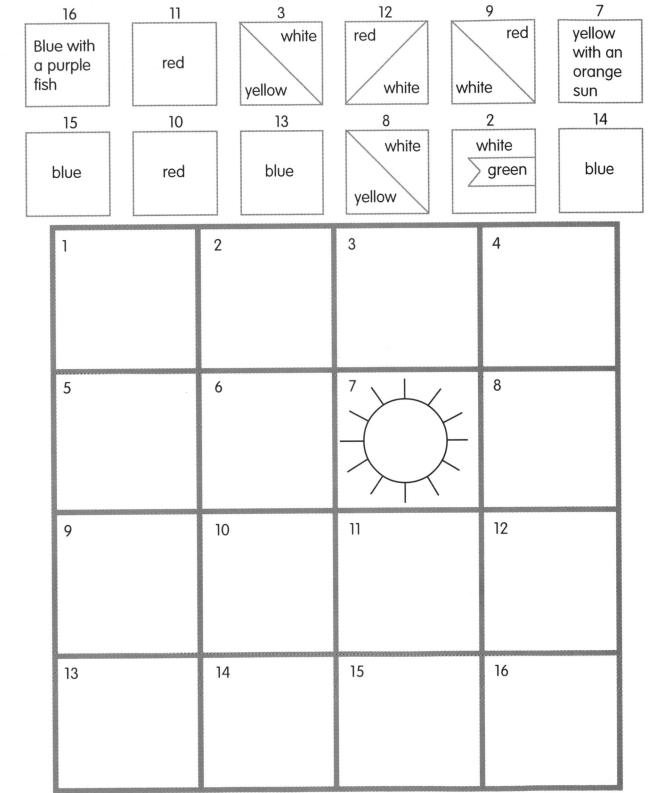

1	2	3	4
5	6	7	8
9	10	11	12
13	14	15	16

Make It

Follow the directions to make a dog.

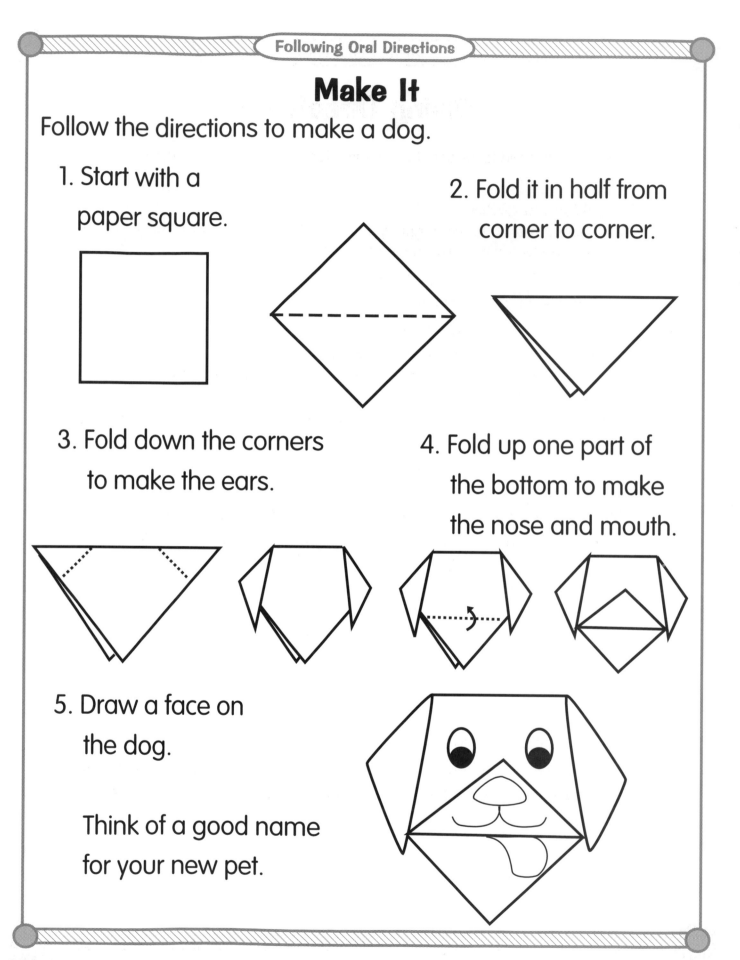

1. Start with a paper square.

2. Fold it in half from corner to corner.

3. Fold down the corners to make the ears.

4. Fold up one part of the bottom to make the nose and mouth.

5. Draw a face on the dog.

Think of a good name for your new pet.

Giving Directions

Young learners need to be able to give directions as well as follow them.

Giving Steps in Order

1. Talk about the importance of giving directions in the correct order. Illustrate this by asking a student to follow these directions:

   > Take your pencil to the pencil sharpener.

   > Turn the handle ten times.

   > Put your pencil in the sharpener.

2. Ask the class to tell you what was wrong with the directions you gave. (They were not in the correct order.) Ask for suggestions about how to give the directions correctly.

3. List words that help us know the order when we give directions - first, second, next, then, last, finally.

Practice Giving Directions

1. Reproduce, laminate, and cut out the direction order words on pages 110-111.

2. Model for the class how to use these words as you give directions. Hold up the order word cards as you give each step.

   ### How to Cut Out a Heart

   > First, fold a square paper in half.

   > Then hold the fold with the hand you don't cut with.

   > Finally, cut around your thumb.

   ### How to "Pump" on the Swings

   > First, push off while sitting on a swing.

   > Second, put your feet out and lean back when the swing moves forward.

   > Last, pull your feet back and lean forward as the swing moves back.

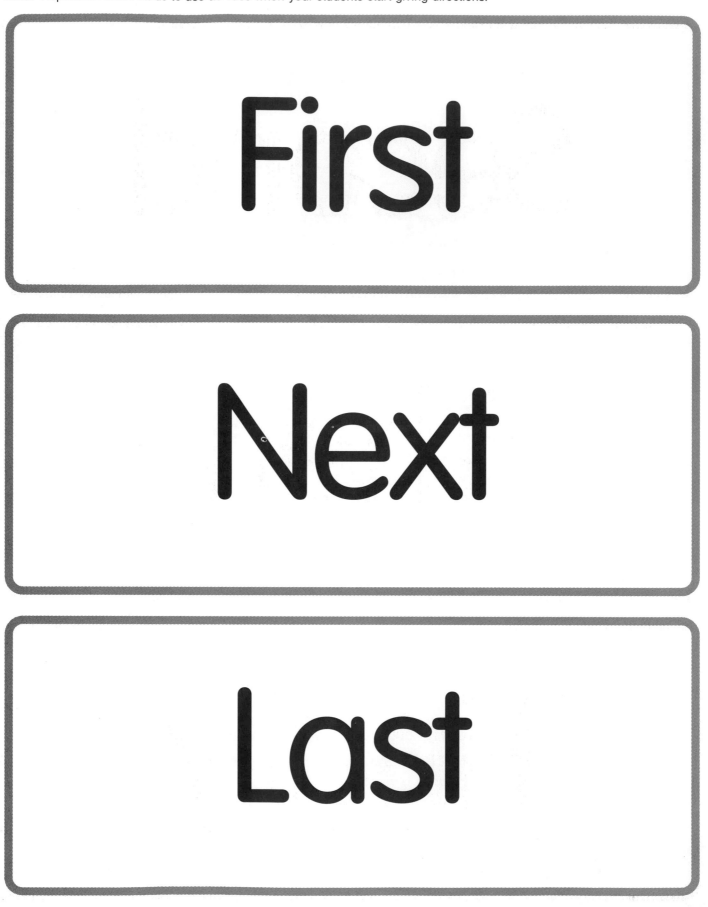

First

Next

Last

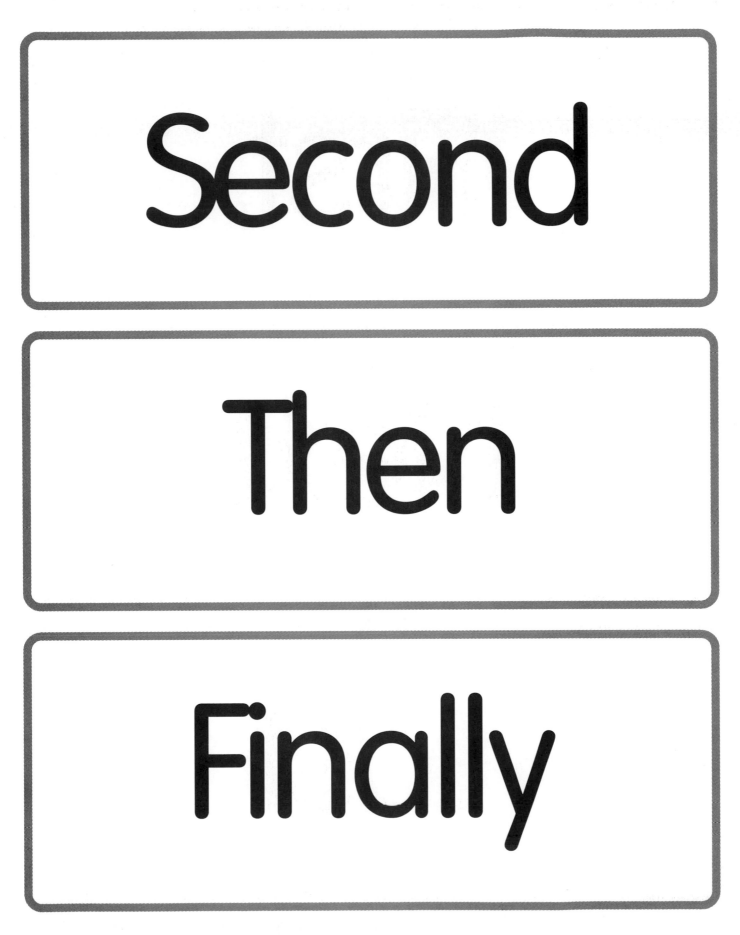

Second

Then

Finally

Following Directions • EMC 738

Pattern Block Shapes

Reproduce these shapes to use with student pages 69 and 70 if you do not have pattern blocks.

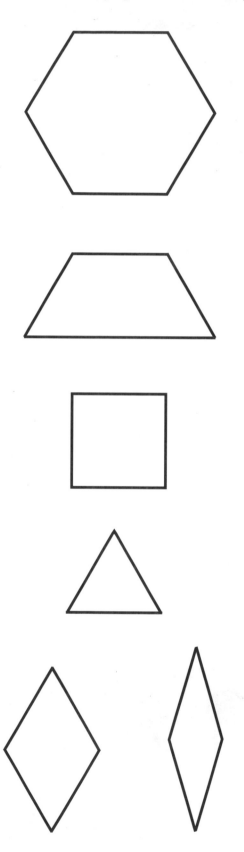

Following Directions • EMC 738